Get Me Through the Next Five Minutes

Also by James Parker

Turned On:
A Biography of Henry Rollins

Get Me through the Next Five Minutes

ODES TO BEING ALIVE

James Parker

W. W. NORTON & COMPANY

Independent Publishers Since 1923

For information about permission to reproduce selections from
this book, write to Permissions, W. W. Norton & Company, Inc.,
500 Fifth Avenue, New York, NY 10110

For information about special discounts for bulk purchases,
please contact W. W. Norton Special Sales at
specialsales@wwnorton.com or 800-233-4830

Manufacturing by Lakeside Book Company
Book design by Patrice Sheridan
Production manager: Julia Druskin

ISBN 978-1-324-09163-9

W. W. Norton & Company, Inc.
500 Fifth Avenue, New York, N.Y. 10110
www.wwnorton.com

W. W. Norton & Company Ltd.
15 Carlisle Street, London W1D 3BS

1 2 3 4 5 6 7 8 9 0

For Kristin Parker
and Harry Parker
and Dr. Cottle
and the Black Seed Writers

All reality is iconoclastic.

—C. S. LEWIS

If God were to appear in my room,
obviously, I would be in awe, but
I don't think I would be humble. I
might cry, but I think he would dig
me like crazy.

—MARC BOLAN

CONTENTS

Get Me Through the Next Five Minutes

INTRODUCTION: THE ODENESS

The Odes came at me.

Back in the sweet innocent summer of 2019, before viruses, before politics, before the sagging iceberg had floated over from Greenland and installed itself in your bathtub, my editors at *The Atlantic* suggested I start doing something regular on the inside back page of the magazine. "Sure thing," I said. "Why don't we call it The Riff? Or The Zoom-In?"

I was imagining a sort of Pollocky prose-explosion, a real showcase/show-off moment for me, the writer. I would *riff*, go cat go. Or I'd *zoom in* with my zany critical lens, bearing down upon and then accelerating through something cultural or political or cultural-political, a joke or a line of poetry or a microphone fail or a note from a guitar solo or . . .

But I wrote some Riffs, and I wrote some Zoom-Ins, and they weren't quite right. They lacked the required surface tension. They lacked, in some cases, a point. "How about we call them Odes?" said my editor John Swansburg. It's nice to work with people who are cleverer than you are.

So the Odes were born, and began to find their nature. Short exercises in gratitude. Or in attention, which may in the end be the same thing. Encounters with the ineffable; encounters with the highly frigging effable. The grace of God; the piece of toast; whatever gets me through the next five minutes. Seeking always what my friend Carlo calls *the odeness*: the essence, the thing of the thing, the quality worth exploring and if possible exalting. Songs of praise, but with (I hoped) a decent amount of complaining in there: a human ratio of moans.

Pindar, they say, Pindar the Greek, he was the ode-originator. His victory hymns for wrestlers, mule racers, and long-distance runners, back in 500 BC, were the first odes. So there's the primary function: celebration. *Check this out.* My Ode to the Unexpected Reversal (about UFC 196) might be considered a kind of upside-down Pindaric ode. But I found I couldn't get on with old Pindar. Hailing the triumph of, say, Theron of Acragas, winner of the chariot race, he would inexplicably (as it seemed to me) overlook the actual charioteering. He'd barely mention the race! No horse-lather, no axle-thunder, no fist-pumping Theron.

Horace, on the other hand, Horace the Roman, I loved: his bantering slightly bitchy tone, his friendly jaundice, his everyday urgency, his very terrestrial odeness. I've Englished, in my own way, a couple of Horace's odes for this book.

Blessed Keats, with his urns and nightingales, used the ode as a ghostly probe, piloting upward or downward through his own consciousness until he was released into the universal. For Pablo Neruda the ode was more like a perceptual Swiss Army knife, for pulling out of your pocket and jimmying your way into the world behind the world. This guy wrote hundreds of odes, loose and straggling and associative and occasionally half-assed, odes to pianos, politicians, socks, fish soup, Machu Picchu, really ranging through the randomness. Many of them were published weekly in the Chilean newspaper *El Nacional*, the poet impressively insisting that they appear not in the arts pages, but alongside the events of the day. Poetry: the latest news on reality.

I had my prose models, too. Chesterton and his essay-things ("On Lying In Bed," "The Advantages of Having One Leg"); Nicholson Baker, ecstatically attentive to the soda-bubbles on a straw in *The Mezzanine*; Mary Gaitskill's wild 1992 paean to Axl Rose ("his rapt, mean little face, the whole turgor of his body"—pure odeness); the continuous ode to excess that was Cintra Wilson's amazing *Critical Shopper* column for *The New York Times*. Loads of stuff. I reread none of it. I don't need that pressure.

The point, I discovered, is that ode-writing is a two-way street. The universe will disclose itself to you, it will give you occasions for odes, it will blaze with interest and appreciability, but you've got to be ode-ready. You've got to bring some twang, some perceptual crispness, some not-worn-out words. Respond to the essence with *your* essence, with the immaculate awareness that is your birthright. And on the days when the immaculate awareness is crap-encrusted, write an ode about that.

As a practice, I can tell you, it gets results. Squirrels treat me differently since I wrote an Ode to Squirrels: they give me the nod, those little fiends. Flight attendants, too. (I salute them in my Ode to Crying While Flying.) I was on a plane to London the other day, in an aisle seat, right next to the flight attendant as he performed the preflight safety demonstration. He was wearing the life vest, he was doing his bit, he was pulling the little toggles and straps with a mild, sighing staginess. And as the tin voice over the PA said "Your life vest also has a whistle and a light for attracting attention," he growled *sotto voce*, with a Scottish accent, "Good luck with *that*."

Has ode-writing improved me, as a person? Refined me, enlarged me, deepened my gratitude? Certainly not. It's true that I'm a little steadier these days. Somewhat less neurotic. But I take this in the spirit of Al Pacino's line from *Carlito's Way*: "You don't get reformed. You just run out of wind."

What *has* improved, though, what has been tuned up by this process, is my eye: I see odes everywhere now. I see them boiling up from the ground where my dog squats to do his business. I see them poking down through the clouds in fingers of divine light. This is a big change for me. Back in the time of Kierkegaard, what with God being recently deceased and Man free-falling through the abyss, it was the philosophical obligation of every vaguely alive person to understand that they were living in secret despair. Today conditions have flipped. Today I'm beginning to think that joy, in the face of everything, is the big secret—that we have a calling, each of us in our own lives, to locate and magnify our hidden or not-so-hidden happiness. And *that's* the odeness.

How about you? There's an ode somewhere in your area right now, I guarantee it. Lurking, tingling. Right next to you maybe. It wants to pull you out of your woolliness and marry you to specificity. It wants to be written, but only by you. There's an everlasting valentine at the nucleus of creation, and it's got your name on it.

Theoretically of course, if one keeps going, ode-writing has the potential to provide a complete—and completely insane—map of the writer's experience: Ode to My Big Toe, Ode to My First Piano Teacher, Ode to My Second Piano Teacher, on and on. A Borgesian nightmare. I've tried to stop well short of that.

There are a couple of odes I haven't been able to write. Ode to Buzz Management, for example, which is my term for the endless business of husbanding one's energies, regulating one's moods, responsibly discharging one's madness, getting excited but not too excited, and so on. I struggled with this for weeks before I realized that this whole book, in a way, is an Ode to Buzz Management. Maybe *everything* is buzz management. Taking exercise, taking drugs, being a hardcore meditator or a hardcore porn addict: all just ways of managing the buzz.

And I really wanted to write an Ode to Lana Del Rey. I have a reverence for Lana Del Rey. I regard her as a shamanic figure, and this ode was going to be my *Waste Land*: a thing of many parts, a floating conspectus of who we are in our heads right now, who we are in America, glimpsed smokily through the vector of Lana's songs and the sleepy wingbeats of her mega-eyelashes. But vaunting ambition did me in, and I choked. Maybe someday.

A word about the poems. If I say that my prose is always on the point of turning into some form of light verse, that's not necessarily a compliment to my prose. But when an Ode felt particularly like it wanted to be a poem, I wrote it as a poem. It will be apparent that I have no fear of doggerel.

Anyway. If you're reading this book in the bathroom, I wish you a hearty peristalsis. If you're reading it on public transportation, look kindly upon your fellow passengers, annoying as they might be. If you're in prison or in the hospital, hang in there. If you're embroiled in a situation, remember Stevie Smith: *All things must pass / Love and mankind are grass.*

And if you're anywhere, anywhere at all, you're alive—and we're in this together.

ODE TO AMERICA

"Pretty good nose you got there! You do much fighting with that nose?"

New Orleans, 1989. I'm standing on a balcony south of the Garden District, and a man—a stranger—is hailing me from the street. He looks like Paul Newman, if Paul Newman was an alcoholic house-painter. I don't, as it happens, do much fighting with this nose, but that's not the point. The point is that something about me, the particular young-man way I'm jutting into the world—physically, attitudinally, beak first—is being recognized. The actual contour of me, or so I feel, is being saluted. For the first time.

America, this is personal. I came to you as a cramped and nervous Brit, an overwound piece of English clockwork, and you laid your cities before me.

The alcoholic housepainter gave me a job, and it worked out pretty much as you might expect, given that I had never painted houses before and he was an alcoholic. Nonetheless I was at large. I was in American space. I could feel it spreading

away unsteadily on either side of me: raw innocence, potential harm, beckoning peaks, fat chasms,
bouncing ions of luck, and threading through it,
in and out of range, fantastic dry-bones laughter.
No safety net anywhere, but rather—if I could only
adjust myself to it, if I could be worthy of it—a
crackling sustaining levity.

I blinked, and the baggage of history fell off me.
Neurosis rolled down the hill. (It rolled back up
later, but that's another story.) America, it's true
what they say about you—all the good stuff. I'd be
allowed to do something here. I'd be encouraged to
do something here. It would be demanded of me,
in the end, that I do something here.

Later that year I'm in San Francisco, ripping up
the carpets in someone's house. Sweaty work. Fun
work, if you don't have to do it all the time: I love
the unzipping sound of a row of carpet tacks pop-
ping out of the hardwood floor. On our lunch
break, my co-ripper and I gaze at the city skyline,
at the shimmering spires, the dewy pavilions of San
Francisco, and I say something about how good I'm
feeling. He turns to me: "Man, you should get paid
just for *that*. They should pay you just for walking around this city with your head up." Only in
America, believe me, do people say things like this.

I've grown up here, in a way. Become a (cough)
man. Driving in America in the early days, I'd

experience a phenomenon I named *Ameripanic*: an overwhelming (for a Brit) apprehension of distance, a kind of horizontal vertigo at the vastness and possibility of this great country. Nausea at the wheel. Called to be Neal Cassady, feeling like Prufrock.

Not anymore. These days, at the wheel in America, I feel sort of—how shall I put it?—*American*. Sort of loose and large-souled. Dunkin' Donuts coffee, elbow out the window, classic rock on the radio . . . You know where you are—wherever you are—with a classic rock station: "Cinnamon Girl," "Sweet Emotion," "War Pigs" . . . It's a liturgy. Somewhere outside New York, on a bright winter morning, the DJ played three Led Zeppelin songs in a row, no commercials—a "Rock Block"—and I lost my mind. I was ecstatic. It was the Led Zepness of driving in America, being in America, the wail and the thrust of it. The world seemed to crack open before me, a Hildegardian egg, a cosmic coal, with a tiny golden Robert Plant squealing like a white-hot Buddha at its core.

So: you fixed me up, America. Now—what can I do for you?

ODE TO THE FARTING HORSE

Three dogs—two golden, one black—are fussing about in a wood.

Rich autumnal vibes: goldenness under the greyness, the exhalation of the aging year. Dead leaves stir on a dry path, trees are demure in their nudity, and the dogs fidget and potter, mouths open: they're agitated. Something's about to happen. Beyond the wood, through an open gate or a gap in the fence, is the green of a meadow.

A crow squawks heraldically, off to the side, and through the gap of green a horse comes cantering in. Sound of his hooves on the path, and the leaf-shuffle of the dogs: the world-skin is tight as a drum. His body is dark brown, his face is sooty black. He comes in fast but with a certain clattery slackness in his gait, half-sideways to his own momentum. His entrance is powerful—head-tossing, hectic, feeling his horsiness—but also quizzical: What's happening in this wood? Who's here?

The dogs are tearing raggedly around, rebounding off the dense and lordly energy of the horse.

The horse, passing close to a fir tree, gives it a flaring kick with his right rear hoof—clonk!—a jolt of pure supremacy, and then slows down. Almost stops. He walks thoughtfully, momentarily nonplussed maybe—why *did* I kick that tree?—turns, regathers the thrust of his horse-being and leaps at or over one of the dogs.

The dog barks; the horse, hindquarters in the air, tail pluming, unzips a couple of disdainful high-pressure farts and thunders back along the path. He exits the wood full tilt, back into the meadow; the dogs follow, the two golden ones keeping pace and the black one trailing stiffly behind.

And that's it. That's all of it—the whole story, twenty-five seconds from beginning to end. It's a YouTube video called "Horse kicks tree, farts on dogs then runs away." Zillions of views.

A human is filming it, obviously—you can hear him making a sort of glugging expectant noise, behind his phone, right at the beginning. And another human, a woman, is glancingly visible as the horse swooshes by her.

But the magic of the video, the reason for its zillions of views, is its non-humanness. It's dogs, a horse, a tree, a space, acting on each other to produce this perfect, and perfectly undesigned, vignette. Everything moves freely. But not chaotically. The laws of nature are observed. And our busy brains are nowhere in there. The horse-cells are doing the thinking. The dog-molecules are doing the thinking. The tree-atoms are doing the thinking. The wood in autumn is doing the thinking.

It's all so random. It's all so beautifully organized.

ODE TO FINDING OUT WHAT
YOU'RE HERE FOR

Why do we love Jason Bourne?

Why does this brooding nobody command our immediate allegiance? Because unlike James Bond, that disgusting collection of appetites and cufflinks, or Jack "Zzzzzzz" Ryan, his mission is not to take down a cartel, destroy an undersea fear factory, or cripple a billion-dollar interstellar weapons system. It's not even to save a beautiful woman. His mission is the essential human mission—*to find out who the hell he is.* And then immediately after that: *what he's for.* "How far then is that wretched and sinful man," John Donne asked his congregation at St. Paul's in June 1622, "from giving any testimony or glory to Christ in his life, who never comes to the knowledge, and consideration, *why* he was sent into this life?"

Bourne, Matt Damon Bourne, the Bourne we know from the movies, was snatched out of the books of Robert Ludlum and substantially rewired by the great screenwriter Tony Gilroy.

Gilroy looked into the character of Bourne, he looked into him with his screenwriter's X-ray eyes, his Hollywood craftsman deep-structure electro-gaze, and what did he see there? He saw *mythos*.

Gilroy's Bourne begins where we all begin, in the absurd condition of man—no idea how he got here, no idea where he's going, but fatally impinged upon by a species of cosmic guilt. Clearly he's meant to be someone—but who? Like Shield Sheaf-son, the Danish king who floats ashore as a baby at the beginning of *Beowulf*, alone and nameless and unprotected, Bourne is an oceanic foundling: out of the water he comes at the beginning of the cycle, plucked unconscious and amnesiac from the Mediterranean, and back into the water (again like Shield Sheafson) he goes at its end, committing himself to the East River with a gorgeous multi-story swan dive.

Pulled from the sea: Jason Bourne, having been dis-covered floating face down on the ocean's bosom, is rebirthed on the wet deck of the Italian fishing boat. He twitches, coughs: the spooked fishermen hiss and draw back. He is tended to—healed—with gruff inexhaustible charity by the ship's doctor. ("I'm a friend!" insists this heroic man, as a pan-icked Bourne rears up and starts choking him. "I am *your* friend!") Recuperating on board, strength-ening, doing chin-ups, Bourne finds himself tying fancy seaman's knots. Hidden skill sets, strange apti-tudes . . . He looks in the mirror and asks himself who he is, in French and then in German. Memory loss? Identity loss—or erasure. A tiny bullet-shaped laser in his hip, pried out by the doctor's scalpel, projects onto the wall an account number from the Gemeinschaft Bank in Zurich, Switzerland. The only clue.

So now Bourne is in Zurich, alone, unknown, past closing time, still wearing the lumpy work clothes given him by the fishermen, framed against blue-lit winter streets. Night falls; his breath rises. A Zurich of the mind. The scene shifts to a small urban park and two Swiss cops on night patrol. Slightly heightened, Narnia-like quality to the setting, snowflakes wheeling down through the aura of a streetlamp. Dreamtime. Bourne is fetal on a park bench, unconscious again; another birth spasm approaches. "Hey!" The cops are rousting him in crisp officious German, telling him to get on his feet, let's go, right now, the park is closed, no sleeping in the park! From their stance, their positioning, the looseness in their shoulders, we infer their readiness to give this nothing-man a beating. Interrogation, flashlight, yellow-white beam in the muddled and sleep-surly face; Bourne shields his eyes. They demand to see his papers, his identification. The question again: Who *is* he? Bourne mumbles, protests groggily that he's lost his papers, first in English and then (as something appears to kick over in his brain, some buried system) in German: *Meine papiere ich habe sie verloren . . .* He looks up sharply, then down again, shaking his head: *Ich muss schlafen.* I must sleep. Let me return to oblivion, be covered up with snow; let me not face again this prodding, peremptory *Who am I?*

You walk to the mailbox, you mail a letter. Walking back, it comes to you with a queer shock of awareness that you have no memory of the mailbox or the act of mailing—and yet the letter is no longer in your hand. You mailed it, as it were, unconsciously. What happens next is the Jason Bourne version of this phenomenon. A nightstick is jabbed into his shoulder: Bourne frowns, as if in recognition. He grabs the nightstick. "Hey!" says the cop. Voltage jump, hair-raising sizzle of imminent violence: the three men are momentarily one circuit. Then Bourne looks right, looks left, stands up and in five movements disarms and dismantles the two cops: *bish bash bosh*, as we say in England. It's over. The letter has been mailed. And the encounter has been reversed: now it's the policemen who are laid out, sleeping in the sleepy snow, while Bourne is all at once horribly conscious, too awake, too aware. It overwhelms him. Panting and confused, he looks at the gun in his hands, breaks it down, drops the pieces, and sprints from the scene.

"Our Hero came from <u>Nowhere</u>—he wasn't going <u>Anywhere</u> and got kicked off <u>Somewhere</u>."

That's the introductory title card of Buster Keaton's *The High Sign*. And Bourne, for all his mystery powers, for all his great seriousness, is now in a kind of Keatonesque slapstick universe. Physics is against him; houses want to fall on him. His ground is unsteady. Anything can happen. Only the dilemma is constant, the not-knowing: Who am I? Who trained me? What *happened* to me?

He appears isolated, attached to nothing, but oh, he's being watched. Bourne is a *subject*. Invisible tiers of surveillance are stacked around this man: CCTV, bugged phones, hacked mainframes, narrow-eyed strangers on street corners muttering into their collars. Angels and demons are watching, the good CIA versus the bad CIA, and his every move sets off a chain reaction across the spook world. Poor Noah Vosen, playing a crooked CIA deputy director in *The Bourne Ultimatum*, spends the entire movie having a shit fit in his information bunker: "What's Bourne doing? Where's he going? Gimme eyes, people! *I need eyes!*"

And how good is Matt Damon, playing Bourne? "You appear to be a mass of contradictions," says Dr. Washburn, the wise old alcoholic in Ludlum's *The Bourne Identity*, examining the memory-wiped Bourne. "There's a subsurface violence almost always in control, but very much alive. There's also a pensiveness that seems painful for you, yet you rarely give vent to the anger that pain must provoke." Isn't that an uncannily spot-on description of Damon-as-Bourne, with the deadness and tristesse in his face, and the arsenal of destruction in his body, stalking about in his black coat like a spare member of Echo and the Bunnymen?

A few years ago I wrote a sequence of poems based on scenes from the Bourne movie franchise. I called them *The Bourne Variations* and I thought I'd invented a new form of critical-lyrical humorous-but-actually-dead-bloody-serious verse. I was quite excited. I hit "Send," sat back and waited for the inevitable storm of acclaim. What I hadn't taken into account was that in order to fully enjoy my poem about, say, the assassination of the journalist Simon Ross at Waterloo Station in *The Bourne Ultimatum*, you had to have just watched *The Bourne Ultimatum*. Like, in the last ten minutes.

Whatever. These are great, glowing-with-mystery movies. Bond is a cipher, Reacher is a monster, Ryan is dull, John Wick . . . I've never seen a John Wick movie . . . but Jason Bourne, poor bastard, poor human suffering the essential questions—he's *one of us*.

ODE TO COMING ROUND

Back at the old grey school, where we all had scuffed shins and hard little minds, there was a brief craze for fainting. It swept through the place like some hot new type of dance. Or was it civil disobedience—a radical going-limp in the face of tyranny? They had us running around, or sitting still, all day: maybe the supreme act of resistance was to switch yourself off.

Morning chapel was the place, at any rate. Morning chapel was Fainting Central. Swoonsville. Sideways City. Eight a.m., leaky grey light, prayers droning skyward, and the pale unbreakfasted boys would sigh and slump from their pews, one after another, in mild reversals of boy energy. Low blood sugar had something to do with it—we were scandalously, I would say almost criminally, underfed. And the hypnotic properties of the prayers themselves, the trance-inducing rhythms, etc., can't be discounted. (*Mystical rose—PRAY for us—Tower of David— PRAY for us—Tower of ivory—PRAY for us . . .*) But basically it was—for a couple of weeks—cool. It was cool to pass out.

Twenty-five years later and the faints were upon me again. Nothing cool about it this time. Now I was in America, a night-shift baker, a freelance journalist, and the father of an infant son. And during those straggle-brained five-a.m. pee trips I found myself fainting rather a lot. Or rather, I found myself on the bathroom floor rather a lot, wondering what had just happened. It was in this phase of my faint-history that I discovered the pleasures of coming round.

Fainting is a disgusting and chaotic experience: everything slips, tips, darkens, crowding greasily towards the omega point, the micro-blip of blackout, and you barely know what's going on.

Coming round, on the other hand, is leisurely and delicious. You feel better, for a start. Measurably improved. The twisted electricity of fainting has discharged itself. And then, oh look, how about this: things, phenomena, are presenting themselves to you gently, in an orderly and unhurried sequence. No rush. Don't get up. Stay right there, you. Plenty of time to appreciate it all—to savour it. How solid the floor beneath you; how cool and smooth the bathroom tiles against your cheek. How generous and unequivocal the clear light of this bathroom. How wonderfully, steadily *actual* the base of the toilet. That stuck-there pubic hair, in its wiry singularity—marvelous.

It passes, of course. This slow-blinking horizontal amazement at the sustaining nature of reality—it fades. Eventually you'll stand up. You'll go wobbling back into your life: it'll get hectic, it'll fall into fragments again. But hang on to the vision if you can, or the aura of it. "Being holds me," said the philosopher and Catholic nun Edith Stein. And on the bathroom floor, just for a moment, you know it: the birds are folded into their nests, the stars are plugged neatly into their outlets, and you—in this world of things—are at home.

ODE TO HOTEL ROOMS

Always different, always the same.

Which is to say, whatever the size or mood or condition of the room, whether there's sinister hair in the bathtub or an orchid in a vase on the table, what greets you as you open the door, every time, is a neutral waft of possibility. A sense of your self-in-waiting. Who are you going to be in *here*? As you mingle with this careful anonymity, as you drift and lightly settle into this fancy or not so fancy non-place, what might happen?

Not much, probably. The old gravity soon asserts itself, the old you-ness; you spread out your things, you follow your patterns, you start making your little habitual messes. You arrive, and then—like delayed luggage—*you* arrive. Somehow the hotel room, in the mystique of its banality, forgives you. Especially if you let housekeeping in. Another day. Another chance. Clean crispy sheets. Your crap politely rearranged. Maybe this time.

Even before you get up to any real mischief, the hotel room invites a minor moral collapse. Your instinct here is to loll, sprawl, degenerate, create crumbs. Unseen hands have laboured for your comfort, and comfort is easily confused with pleasure. So you go slightly vicious. You want to drink the citrus body wash. You want to fry yourself on the free Wi-Fi.

I do love the noises. Whine or wheeze of the bathroom fan; bovine thuds in the hallway; the minibar clicking on as you lie there in bed, and then that strange carpety breathlessness in the air—quintessence of insomnia—after it clicks off. Those muffled voices through the wall, the low honking incomprehensible vowels, the cello-like groans—surely they recall the experience of being in the womb? What are the grown-ups *doing*, on the other side of the membrane?

And then it's over. Checkout comes galloping, always too fast, and now all of a sudden you have to get it together: your stuff, your brain. You're trapped in a time-lapse movie about yourself, packing. What happened in here, anyway? Was it good or bad? Hustle, hustle, and don't forget to leave a nice tip for the cleaners. Propitiate the hotel room, because you'll be back. On another day, in another city, somewhere inside the eternally hanging dream honeycomb of hotel rooms, a lock will unclick. Wide-eyed with expectation, you'll open another door.

ODE TO INSUFFICIENCY

I made my ghost
a piece of toast
and asked which jam he liked the most.
My ghost said he liked apricot.
And I said "Damn.
That's the one kind of jam
I haven't got."

ODE TO TAKING IT SERIOUSLY

As a drummer, sure, I've got problems.

Wobbly right foot; sloppy left hand; misdirected strike-power, such that my kit will literally fly apart when we play a show, expanding in all directions like the universe.

But. BUT. Moody with drum-doubt as I often am, preoccupied as I may be by my own shortcomings, for our *collective* thing, for who we are as a *band*, I have nothing but an idolatrous passion. I can't believe how good we are. We sound, when we're in our groove, like REM's *Murmur* performed by some very talented walruses. We sound like Neil Young falling out of bed. We sound like five middle-aged men slurping with wild gratitude at the elixir of rock'n'roll. Which weirdly—we are discovering—makes you older, not younger. But so what?

I once—for an article I was writing—spent a weekend in Vermont with some Revolutionary War reenactors. We were all in our itchy period gear, refighting the Battle of Hubbardton. And I liked them, the reenactors, but as one of them came to the end of an especially fervent monologue about tactics or musketry or buttons I asked him if he wasn't perhaps taking it all a bit seriously. He looked at me with the transparency of the Dalai Lama. "The more seriously you take it," he said, "the more fun it is."

So with life, so with being in a band. An earnest commitment at ground level gets you access to the higher playfulness. We practice hard in my band; we take pains. We fuss over parts. We have sudden bold ideas. Greg, rhythm guitarist/songwriter, expresses himself deeply and purely through our music. ("When I discovered the key of G," he told us once, during practice, "that's when this whole thing popped open.") And in Greg's basement we are all in the grip of the same late-flowering love. Our lives and responsibilities pile up outside. In rock'n'roll terms, we refight the Battle of Hubbardton every week.

And if you practice enough, you can stop thinking. Which is bliss. In the heart of the noise there's a silent click of abandonment, and you're away. Look at me: released from the oppression of cogitation, bouncing off my drums. Nor am I alone. I'm with my friends, who before my suddenly cleared eyes are assuming their flame-like Platonic forms. There's George, head down, shaking torrents of noise out of his guitar. There's Mark the singer: his tambourine scatters sparks. There's Scott, rebirthed every four bars by the all-mothering rumble of his bass playing. We blend, mingle, lose our outlines. (This feeling, I came to understand in Greg's basement, is why musicians take drugs. They have to! Because it's fleeting, and when it's gone it's gone, and maybe nothing in ordinary life can touch it.)

Are we going anywhere, as a unit? Are we wasting our time? We've got haggard faces and haggard minds: when we make an album, we're calling it *Look What Happens to People*. This half-daft endeavour, our bonfire of the dad-rockers—it's real. "Eternity is in love with the productions of Time," said William Blake. Heads down, fuckers. Try hard. Get better. Take it seriously, and you'll be the envy of the angels.

ODE TO BALLOONS

There are balloons and then there are balloons.

There's the domestic balloon, over which we shall quickly pass: the dull little balloon that you blow up at home, for a party, with your own laborious lungfuls of why-the-fuck-am-I-doing-this carbon dioxide. A lot of pathos, for whatever reason, attaches to this balloon.

Then there's the taut and shining helium balloon that you buy in the shops. A balloon of this sort is essentially arrested upthrust. A trapped *alleluia*, if you like, the thwarted attempt of a single bubble of helium, that vivacious gas, to fly into heaven and diffuse itself in eternal joy. We're tethering this balloon, we're holding it down, we're interfering with its purpose, but the balloon doesn't care. Brainless and glorious it bobs about. Life is heavy, heavy, heavy. Since we crawled up groaning onto dry land, gravity has been patiently dismantling us— we sag, we stoop, our earlobes droop, our lower backs hurt. Experience accumulates, and it has its own weight. Bring on the balloons.

I love the balloons that float like deities above the aisles in CVS or Star Market; the balloons made of Mylar and imagination. These balloons have special powers. These balloons, out in the world, will activate gratuitous nonmalignant forces. They'll get you smiles, fist bumps, kisses, drinks. I once walked several blocks with a large Sponge-Bob SquarePants balloon surging and tugging over my head. People cried out, reflexively—they were glad to see him. (That balloon later escaped; I watched SpongeBob recede, grinning, into the blue-eyed void of the sky.)

I've been hauling balloons into my apartment recently, great gaggles of them, in the interest of general mood elevation. There have been occasions, too, moments to mark: birthdays, graduations, whatever. They're over now. But the balloons remain—glimmering, immaterial. A flamingo; a sunflower; a foaming beer; a gigantic golden replica of the thumbs-up emoji. The balloon I bought myself on Father's Day: BEST DAD EVER. (Superlatives: this is balloon language.) My wife says these balloons satisfy my "need for cheese"—which is to say, my low consumer attraction to things that are bright, things that jiggle.

But to me the balloons are like Yeats's wild swans at Coole: "mysterious, beautiful." Or like Jeeves the butler at his most silvery and wafting. They travel unaccountably from room to room, trailing their strings. They nudge me at my desk. They drift together, and nod, and seem to confer: a symposium of balloons. They touch one another so gently.

ODE TO GETTING RID
OF THE ALBATROSS

How do you get the albatross off your neck?

You know, *your* albatross. Your own dank collar of
bird carcass, bespoke feathery deadweight of shame/
rage/neurosis/solipsism/the past/whatever, the
price of being *you* as it feels on a bad day . . . How
do you let it drop?

Samuel Taylor Coleridge was very clear on this:
you bless the water snakes. It's all in Part IV of
The Rime of the Ancient Mariner, the greatest poem
ever written.

The ship is becalmed, the sea is rancid, the crew are
dead, and the Mariner—albatross slung Bjork-ishly
around his neck—is sitting on the deck in a state of
nightmare. Meaning, purpose, a following wind:
all gone. Perished with his shipmates. Now he's in
a scummy realm, a realm of mere biological outlast-
ing. "A thousand thousand slimy things lived on /
And so did I . . ."

But. However. And yet. With nothing else to do,
with no phone to look at, he watches the slimy

things as they writhe and flare in the water, super-white in the moonlight, darker and more luxuriously hued when in the shadow cast by the ship itself. And something happens. His heart opens. Or perhaps it breaks. He is mutely, selflessly, stirred and awakened. With his core, from his core, he spontaneously exalts what is before him: he blesses the water snakes.

And with a complicated downy loosening, and maybe a glancing clang from its beak, the albatross—fatal baggage of a bird—falls off. Into the sea.

To feel the rush of this moment, the heavy metal emancipation of it, I do recommend Iron Maiden's "Rime of the Ancient Mariner." The live version, preferably. This is a straight-up workingman's adaptation of the poem, fourteen minutes of galumphing rock opera, Coleridge's words doggedly paraphrased by Maiden bassist/vision guy Steve Harris, and it succeeds spectacularly. Especially at the water-snakes moment, which the band orchestrates to perfection: a flicked and rushing pattern on the hi-hat, a trebley-warbley melodic figure on the bass, palm-muted chug-a-chug of one, then two (then three?) guitars, the tension blissfully building until Bruce Dickinson, with soaring all-gobbling theatricality, sings it out. Yes. The spell is broken. The albatross falls from his neck.

So what *are* the water snakes? Coleridge's *Rime* is not an allegory, so the water snakes are not representing or symbolizing something. They *are* something. A coiling and uncoiling beautiful-terrible, playful-awful force that breaks the surface in snaky loops and flashes. Wonderfully indifferent to us, horrifyingly indifferent to us. But mysteriously in relationship with us, because it is in our eyes that these water snakes, these incandescent eels, these limbless creatures of the deep, are made holy. We are the ones who can bless them.

And you can't *decide* to bless the water snakes, that's the point. It's not gratitude. It's not about improving your mental health. No squint of effort, no knotting or unknotting of the frontal lobes will get you there. The blessing arises by itself, or it doesn't arise at all. Total brain bypass: a love so simple and helpless it barely even knows what it's loving.

So it becomes a question of orienting oneself to the possibility of this love. How to do it? I'm out of my depth here—which is just as it should be, for here we are in the zone of the mystics and the mega-meditators. We are full fathom five, where your feet don't touch anything because there's nothing to touch. If you're the Ancient Mariner—or perhaps if you're addicted to opiates, as Coleridge was—you'll have to go through it, all of it. You'll have to be carried to the end of yourself. The blessing of the water snakes happens at the Mariner's clinical bottoming-out: when he's utterly isolated, on a suppurating sea, besieged by the forces of death.

The rest of us, maybe we don't have to go—or be taken—that far. Maybe there are other, less drastic, more everyday opportunities and invitations for us to be broken down and opened up. For our grip on the albatross to be unclenched. For the love to pour through us like Iron Maiden. One way or another, though, sooner or later, gently or with loud sunderings and burstings, it's going to happen.

Life, thank God, it'll get you and get you again.

ODE TO MEDITATION

Think no thoughts.
Let all the brain's productions be
a flow of shining noughts.
Be still.
Stillness is a thrill.
Say nothing to yourself. Let words
lie flat like tingling swords.
Put sex away.
You'll attend to the itch in the underpants
another day.

(At this point,
should you find yourself
in a warehouse of mental din,
pursued by a grinning zilch,
with two ravens tugging at your intestines,
one going one way, one going the other,
and a red phallus rising before you, mute
    as an idol,

congratulations: you're meditating.)

ODE TO THE RIGHT ART
AT THE RIGHT TIME

The classroom smelled of dryness and quelled rage. Mice bowled their turds across it by night. The headmaster had nostrils like inverted cauldrons and moved heavily down the poorly lit corridors. His tread was fateful: his temper imprisoned us. During lessons I drew a lot of doodles of this man being torn apart by wild horses, or having his mouth stuffed with sticks of dynamite.

We feared homesickness like the bubonic plague. Boys who caught it—that horrifyingly complete sorrow, that sorrow that empties out your whole body—would be shunned. You'd know them by their white, wet faces and the fact that they were always alone. If one of these boys, in the dark dormitory, after lights-out, started snuffling with helpless misery, we'd throw our slippers at him.

Like a lot of English boarding schools, the place was a repurposed stately home: a grey pile in the countryside, a shell, a great house gone to seed, a hulk of collapsed aristocracy turned bare-bones commercial by the now-unwealthy family. The teachers had been recruited, it seemed to us, on

the anti–*Magnificent Seven* principle. You're familiar with *The Magnificent Seven*? A 1960 Western
knockoff of Kurosawa's *Seven Samurai*, this was the
greatest movie we had ever seen, completely sat-
isfying our incredible thirst for justice. Mexican
villagers, oppressed by leering, bullying bandits,
hire a crew of mercenary master gunmen to help
them fight back. One by one they are located,
these lethal aces—sought out and signed up for
the gig. James Coburn, ice-cold knife thrower,
is found dozing against a fencepost with his hat
over his eyes; mighty Charles Bronson, when
they track *him* down, is working off his surplus
murder-energy by chopping a huge pile of wood;
and so on.

You see where I'm going with this. The teachers at
our boarding school on the wet plains of Suffolk, the
body of men to whom our welfare was entrusted,
appeared to have been assembled, headhunted, on
the opposite principle. The anti–*Magnificent Seven*
principle. One of them had perhaps been spotted in
a northern town, getting thrown off a bus; another,
hiding trouserless in a broom cupboard in the British Library. Halfway houses, cracked infirmaries,
mouldy bed-and-breakfasts and the backs of old
pubs up and down the country had been scoured,
turned over, for the absolute worst. The maddest
and least capable specimens. And now here they all
were, hired and installed. With us.

Am I being merely flippant? Do I exaggerate? When I consult my nine-year-old self, I find that I exaggerate not at all. My hatred for some of these men was one of the most sanctified emotions of my young life: a hatred, as Henry Rollins wrote somewhere, "pure as sunshine." For some of the others I had pity—the special merciless pity of a child—and one or two, amazingly, I liked.

We, the inmates, victimized one another relentlessly. No exemplary characters here, no noble schoolboys, no one to emulate. The environment devoured itself—and kept on munching. And I was small, and threatened by everybody, with a neurological aversion to mud, cold, roughness, shouting, obscenity—the very textures of English boarding school life. So I had to go verbal. Good at jokes, good at stories; also good at taunts and nicknames, and putdowns, and mockeries that sharpened with repetition. (Later, grown-up and remorseful, I would anxiously scan my writing for traces of the ancient meanness, the mark of the beast. One reason English critic-types tend do well in America, I think: we come pretrained in being horrible.)

I did something interesting, though. Fluent little fucker that I was, I took the unusual step of developing a stammer. Not a stutter, where you repeat the beginning of a word, clicking and bouncing, but a *stammer*: You seize up. Nothing comes out.

That's how I define the difference anyway: with a stutter, you utter, however imperfectly, but with a stammer, you're jammed. Pure shoved-down anger, it seems to me now. Wrath backfired into the brain-stem. Stuck in a stammer, with the blocked syllable bulging behind my eyes, I would feel literally explosive: now it was *my* mouth stuffed with dynamite. What if I SPOKE it?

Teachers, especially, could make me self-thwart like this. But also doctors, policemen, shopkeepers, receptionists, bouncers, waiters, plumbers, girls, any kind of staged situation, anyone at a desk or a door, anyone for whom I was obliged to prepare a question, anyone to whom I might be expected to give an even momentary account of myself. It still happens now and again. The other day in the grocery store, addressing a woman at the deli counter, I made a tired and stammery mess of the line *Could I have half a pound of the turkey, please?* She looked at me levelly over her silver slicer. "You can have it if you can say it," she said. I laughed: "Ah . . . One of those days." "I hear you," she said.

It wasn't all bad at that school. I was also a boy, a child, with a child's original still-wrigglingly-connected consciousness. So along with all the terrors and the nastiness there were the tumbling ecstasies, the heroic presentiments, the ultra-vivid details, the interior panoramas, the feelings that pushed out in waves toward the horizon. My two brothers were there with me. And because we *lived* there, we had a weird amount of freedom: we spent a lot of time building fires in the woods, or wandering rhapsodically along the edge of the playing field, or thrashing with sticks the huge woolly grove of grey-green nettles (nettles: ancestral herbal enemy of all schoolboys) that had grown over the disused orchard.

And I had art. Poetry: Betjeman, Hopkins, Yeats, Dylan Thomas, the War poets (how I worshipped, still do, the War poets). Music: the Jam, the Police, Adam and the Ants, ABBA.

But most of all I had *The Wall*.

December 1979: My mother, with wonderful maternal practicality, seeks a recommendation from the groovy young man at the local hi-fi shop. Her son likes pop music, so what should she give him for Christmas? Ah, says the groovy young man, *well*. Pink Floyd have just released a rather remarkable album . . . And so it came into my hands, as a clunky double cassette, this amazing opus, this dripping severed lump of the English psyche: *The Wall*.

Stylistically, for me, *The Wall* was a universe. It seemed to contain all known music, everything I had heard and would ever hear, from Weillesque showtunes to paranoid soft-rock ballads to near-metal to the queasy disco of the big hit, "Another

Brick in the Wall Pt. 2." There was no punk rock in there because it was all punk rock: The sneering, the satire, the atmosphere of persecution and breakdown. Muttered or snarling or wailing adult voices. Things being smashed. Loads of post–John Martyn looping reverb on the guitar, suggestive of memory layers and dissolving identities.

The Walkman hadn't yet been invented. I was wired up to *The Wall* via a single medical-looking off-white earpiece, which connected to the black-and-silver brick of my precious Sony cassette recorder. I heard the whole thing, that is, through one overworked ear. And how passionately I attended to that etiolated signal. I was like Proust in his in his cork-lined apartment in Paris, listening to a live performance of Debussy's *Pélleas et Mélisande* down the crackly line of his *théâtrophone*.

The Wall is a concept album. It has a plot. Most concept albums lose the plot, because musicians take too many drugs to think a thing through. Not *The Wall*. Roger Waters, Pink Floyd's grumpy-face genius, keeps it tight. A boy without a father— killed in the war—goes to school, is tyrannized by loony teachers, grows up to be some kind of satanic audience-despising rock star, and finally detonates in overlord madness, screaming about Britannia and cleaning up the streets. And the master metaphor, of course, is THE WALL: the wall of conditioning, repression, manners, schooling, stultification, false selfhood, Englishness. I got most of this, or pre-got it (I was only eleven) but for me the wall meant one immediate thing: my stammer. Somehow, in my speech, I'd got myself blockaded. Bricked-in. The wall ran right across my tongue.

Miraculous, how we seem to get the art we need, at the moment that we need it. My stammer, these days, is vestigial. A tiny glitch or hiccup, a bizarre word-choice, a flicker in the eyes. But I'll never grow out of *The Wall*. This is the album that came in through one side of my head, carrying the truth like a prophecy. Because the wall was going up around me, sure as bricks are bricks. And behind it, like a giant stammer, the pressure would build.

ODE TO GIVING PEOPLE MONEY

It's a primal scene, a biblical scene: the have meets the have-not. In the subway, on the street, at the traffic light, along the underpass, anywhere in America. Abundance—as in an experiment in moral physics—is confronted by lack. What happens next?

You, patently, have. A bed, a shower, a fridge, a place to go, a buffer or two against intolerable pressure. The person in front of you, patently, has not. A glance suffices to tell you that. And they're asking you for money. Do you give it? Should you? Must you? Do you *want* to?

We can dispense immediately with the traditional canard: *they'll only spend it on drugs.* Fuck—if I may—that. What a pernicious mingling of Ayn Randian superiority and liberal pseudo-concern. As Jerry says to George in an episode of *Seinfeld*: "Are you even vaguely familiar with the concept of giving?" Maybe they will spend it on drugs. Or maybe they'll spend it on a new copy of William James's *The Varieties of Religious Experience,* to replace the one that was lost when their campsite of two years was deconstructed—in their absence—by park rangers. The point is, you don't know. And if you've truly *given*, it's none of your business.

Let's get back to the encounter itself. Awkward, isn't it? The society of which you have just been correctly identified as a member, the system of which you are a functioning part, has thrown the person before you into a transparent condition of penury and exile. What sets you up has broken them down. What swallows you has spat them out. Perhaps you feel a flickering of shame. And then a flickering of annoyance at the flickering of shame. Jesus Christ, their hands are out and their tin cups are rattling—why can't they leave you alone? Affluence is no picnic: you have a prescription to refill, a phone to upgrade, a car to get repaired, a spouse to argue with. This endless suck of ambient need—it's too much.

Here's my tip: if you're temperamentally indisposed, keep your money. A penny given a poor man "grudgingly," wrote the magnificent nutter Leon Bloy, "pierces the poor man's hand, falls, pierces the earth, bores holes in suns, crosses the firmament and compromises the universe." So don't do that.

But if you *are* inclined to give, then give wholeheartedly. Not for charity, not for responsibility, not even for the person in front of you, but for the act itself. Existence is a gift, right? You don't have to like it, but it's a gift. A cosmic freebie. And when you give, unconditionally, you're participating in the same divine economy that big-banged you—*you*— into being. Let it circulate through you unobstructed. Through your glands and through your veins. The person before you needs money, and you need to give it. Unplug the springs of life, and hand it over.

ODE TO THE PANDEMIC

I met a traveler from an antique land
who stopped me with a blue-gloved hand
and said, "That's close enough.
You might be carrying viral lint in your
    trouser cuff."

I could tell from the smell in the room
he'd been having sex on Zoom.
It was a shame we were so out of phase.
It was a shame we met in these dog days.
The parks are brown.
The rich are out of town.
I walk across Boston Common, forgetting
    people's names,
and one by one behind me the trees burst
    into flames.

ODE TO BRAIN FARTS

Whistling synapses. Dead sparks launched from the neurotransmitters. Dismay, and a kind of terror at the blankness.

Let's attempt a taxonomy here. There's the brain fart of *technique*: abrupt incompetence, the wild bungling or buggering-up of something you're usually good at. There's the brain fart of *memory*: the flying-away, even as you mentally reach for it, of your PIN number, the name of your favourite restaurant, the name of your friend's wife. There's the brain fart of *intellect*: the terrible idea that, for an inexplicable brain-farty moment, seems like a brilliant idea.

And then, perhaps most alarming, there's the brain fart of *being*: The whoosh, sudden as falling down an open manhole, of not-knowing-who-you-are-or-what-you're-doing. Of barely knowing your own name. The swat of nonentity, cat's-paw quick. I get about three of these a week.

Brain fart. Superb piece of nomenclature. A bleb of nothing-gas, a minor release, like a smoke-ring from the mouth of a little demon, dilating in a wavering zero over your consciousness. You had something, you knew something, you were something, and now it's gone. In its place is just this whiff of removal, slightly mephitic: brain fart.

Be forgiving of your brain farts. After what feels like an egregious brain fart of memory, for example, I might soothe myself thus: *Dude, you're pretty solid on heavy metal drummers, seventeenth-century poets and plotlines from* Seinfeld. *You have vast non-overlapping fields of semi-expertise. Is it really so awful that you've momentarily mislaid the name of that fullback for Real Madrid, the one who almost pulled Mo Salah's arm off in the 2018 Champions League Final?* (Answer: Sergio Ramos.)

Appreciate them, if you can. Each brain fart is a nonsense-holiday, a mini-break in meaninglessness. The proximity of chaos; the fragility of the web of recognitions. It's worth being reminded of these things. Take your dose of confusion like medicine. Maybe even enjoy it. There's buoyancy in a brain fart. Float or hover on the absence of content.

Besides, we always figure it out, don't we? The PIN number comes wafting back to us; we recognize, eventually, the terribleness of the terrible idea. We remember our own names. And if not . . . Well, maybe it's time to be somebody else.

ODE TO CRYING BABIES

Crying baby, I hear you.

I've got no choice but to hear you. You're ten rows ahead of me in Economy, raging like Lear on the heath. *Blow, winds, and crack your cheeks!* You're challenging the gods, the elements, the injustice of life. You may also have gas.

Who is by your side, as you arraign the universal order? Who is with you at this ultimate moment? Lear had his Fool, and you have your parents. Pale, stretched, stooping presences. They loom over you uncertainly. Exhaustedly. Most horrible, with the last of their energy, they *bicker*: even as they attend to you, they're saying quietly vile things to each other. If they get divorced, crying baby, it's your fault.

But listen: I appreciate you. I appreciate your outspokenness. Your indignation. These bodies that we're in, they're not always the greatest, are they? They itch, they sting, they ache, they bloat, they overheat. They feel weird. They get tired. They make us grumpy. Which is, now I think about it, another thing I appreciate about you: with you, the rusty old mind/body binary does not apply. You're pure mood. Or pure biology. Your digestive system and your emotional life are basically the same thing.

My own days as a crying baby I have forgotten. (How does that happen? Where do we stash those great seasons of rage? Those unmatched ego flights?) But I do remember when I lived with one. He's twenty-one now. The bitter clarion of his voice in the night would rouse me like an electric shock.

Anyway—keep it up, little tyrant. These crescendoes, these arcs of noise. These cluckings, incensed silences and long shivering notes. You've got a lot of power, and you've got no power at all. You're a tiny fist shaken at the heavens. Soon you'll be talking, and language will betray you. You'll utter vague helpless half-sentences. You'll make bad jokes. But right now your voice is very direct, very effective. It's going right through my head.

ODE TO CHEWING GUM

Ever broken a piece of gum?

Broken its spirit, I mean. Chewed it for so long, and with such absent-minded mechanical fury, that it finally gives up. It snaps. Its molecular structure collapses and it dissolves into a kind of traumatized putty in your mouth. I've only done this once in my life, after a night of dance floors and chemicals in London, but it impressed me greatly.

First I was impressed with myself, the up-all-night masticating lunatic. Nice one, kid. Such wonderful aimless energy!

Then I began to think about the piece of gum. Its elasticity. Its resilience. How many hours of thoughtless gnashing had it given me before I killed it with my power-jaws? Its tiny dowry of flavour— spearmint? cinnamon?—was exhausted in the first five minutes; after that it was pure endurance, pure interior technology, shifting and resisting, on and on until dawn rose whitely and *everything* sort of fell to pieces. End of the night . . . That broken-gum, party's-over moment. You look around you:

the dance floor is full of nutters, twitching, green with sweat. They're not your brothers and sisters. Reality drizzles, then pours in. Greyness floods the skylights of the mind.

Gum is not exactly a handmaiden to the arts—it's not opium or Earl Grey—but it does enhance concentration. It helps you get on with things. Maybe because it feels almost autonomic, like something our body is taking care of without us; the act of chewing-for-the-sake-of-chewing smoothes out anxiety and irrigates the brain. "Dad," my son asked me last week, "do you think you have ADD?" No, I said, but I *am* quite lazy. If the choice is between two hours of rapturous flow-state composition and a forty-third viewing of *Scent of a Woman*, I'll pick the latter. So I need my gum. It lets me know I'm working.

Of course, once it's served its purpose, it's rather disgusting. Used gum, chewed gum. *What I do is me: for that I came*, wrote Gerard Manley Hopkins, a huge fan of Trident Original Flavor. And gum's grand refusal to surrender its form, to melt away or decompose, to be anything but what it is, becomes in the end a bit of a problem. How to dispose of it? Me, I like to throw it from the window of a moving vehicle. Not really a long-term solution.

Someone told me at school that if you swallowed a piece of gum it would wrap itself around your heart. Amazing image. So chew on, humans. Those knobs or wads of used gum, with their genital shapes—they're tiny monuments to contemplation, really. Each one memorializes a distinct passage of mind. The thoughts are flown, but the gum remains. Get it on your shoe, wrap it round your heart, and think of me.

ODE TO THE PSYCHEDELIC
LOCUSTS THAT RUN THE UNIVERSE

I don't actually believe in them. But I know they're out there.

I know that if I took the right/wrong drugs, or had a psychotic break, or watched too many episodes of *Rick & Morty*, I'd see them. I know they'd manifest, looming before me like an alien priesthood. Nine feet tall, Gigeresque, rustling and chittering and grating the plates of their armour: the psychedelic locusts that run the universe.

Is my not believing in them a precondition of their existence? Is my unbelief the guarantor of their locust supremacy? Maybe. I blame them for everything. They invented Facebook, smooth jazz, passive aggression, and the dazzle of deadness you get from an LED lightbulb. In their control room behind the stars, in the deep backstage of the cosmic drama, that's where you'll find them. Standing around. Grinding their forelegs. Woggling their antennae. Leering at banks of screens and coldly generating the situations that we—poor bastard humanity—must live through.

And the situations are getting slightly worse.
Because they're locusts.

That bad-TV feeling we've all been getting, that
we're in the spin-off of a spin-off and about to
get cancelled mid-season? That's them! That's the
locusts. That glare of indifference you exchanged,
just this morning, with an unknown somebody on
the subway? The locusts again. That strange suction
of quiet in your kitchen after the fridge clicks off?
Slightly brain-destroying? *Locusts.*

They feast on isolation, on separation. Human
loneliness is their champagne. Up in the command
center, right now, they're gloating over their con-
soles. They're creaking with icy glee.

Love alone will defeat them.

ODE TO MY DOG'S BALLS

We couldn't take them from him.

No, we couldn't do it. For Sonny the dog, castration was never an option. Nothing ideological about it—I know there are trainers and dog-types who will advocate for an "intact" animal, but this was a purely emotional analysis.

Sonny came to us from India, from the streets of Delhi, and the various ruptures and dislocations involved in getting him to our apartment had left him quivering, volatile, tender, spooked, curved in on himself, Ringo-Starr-eyed, a little morbid and damp of soul. He arrived in January, in the glassy blue heart of a Massachusetts winter, and every cold-clarified sound on our street—cough/clunk of a car door closing, sharp tingle of keys—made him jump. My wife said that taking him for a walk in those early days was like tripping on LSD. If we removed his balls (we felt) that would be the end of his personality: he'd curl up and blow away like a dead leaf.

Like I said, emotional. Non-rational. We should have neutered him, but—we didn't. So . . .

So he retains them, grandly and purply: his testes, his tokens, his clangers, his plums. And because of them, he gets a lot of grief in the neighbourhood. And I mean a LOT. Male dogs, with rare and shining exceptions, are outraged by him. They just cannot believe it, his free-swinging, low-hanging, full-bollocked lifestyle. The effrontery of it. It drives them out of their minds. From behind the windows of houses and apartment buildings they roar at him, scrabbling at the glass or throwing themselves against it with furry thumps; from porches and balconies they shriek at him; on the street they snuffle with fury, they stand on their hind legs and choke on their leashes, desperate to fight. They hate the sight of Sonny. They hate the sight of me, walking Sonny. So wherever we go, in addition to the squawks of the dog-detesting squirrels in their trees, we must suffer the heckling of the local *castrati*. Hostile world.

Am I overstating it a bit? Subjectively speaking, not at all. Boston is a port city, with gulls in the air, and sometimes I think even those gulls are against us—those wheeling, vituperating seagulls.

By breed, Sonny is a Pariah or Desi dog, slender, keen and honey-coloured, around thirty-five pounds, with a narrow ribcage and flayed,

Iggy Pop–like musculature. One of the ur-dogs of the planet, a dingo/jackal/hound, a traveller-in-packs, a sharp-witted middleweight, superfast runner, beaky, brainy, built for the Great Unravelling, for broken cities and despairing populations. He is *Canis canis*, God's mongrel and ultimately-boiled-down compound animal: if all the dogs in the world (I like saying this to fellow dog-owners) had sex with all the other dogs, you'd end up with a dog like Sonny.

In his person he combines great elegance with something lowdown and trash-inflected and all-surviving. He has a dainty, floaty way of walking, a faun-like delicacy of limb, and an aesthetic approach to taking a shit. He has an affinity for ramps, alleys, doorways, neglected corners, loading bays, back areas: in these non-places he looks very briefly at home. He is deeply suspicious, wildly alert and absolutely reverent of reality. People who live on the street tend to greet him with a kind of recognition.

At first he wouldn't even walk with me. On the sidewalk, mid-stride, he'd stop, stiffen his forelegs, dip his head, and glower at me with a combination of sunken defiance and great sadness. The leash did not connect us—no, it divided us cruelly. Once in the early days I tried to take him to the liquor store (a man and his dog go to buy some whiskey—what could be nicer?) and he balked on the leash after half a block. Dug in, bunched up, wouldn't move. The truculent stare. I cursed. I pulled. I wheedled. Nothing happened. We returned home, alienated (him) and furious (me.) "Fuck it!" I said. "I can do without whiskey." "You sure about that?" said my son. (Thirteen at the time.)

It took a while to build trust. Months passed before Sonny would truly meet my eye. Long months for me: I'd stick my face hotly into his, looking for love. There's an endorphin released (or so I'd been reading) by the infatuated, beseeching gaze of one's dog. I had to have it. Was it down there somewhere, deep in the seas of his eyeball, could I find it: LOVE? Love to twitch the neurochemical trigger and give me the juicy endorphins? No chance. No love for me, or not yet. Sonny, with an oppressed air, would look steadily away. Neediness offends him.

It was in this era of our relationship that I would often despairingly, and to my wife's mounting annoyance, quote a line from J. R. Ackerley's *My Dog Tulip*: "Alas for the gulf between man and beast!"

Incidentally, if you're picking up a note of strain or excess from my writing about Sonny, that's because I'm having an Oedipal style–struggle with J. R. Ackerley. I confess it and I can't help it. *My Dog Tulip*, in which Ackerley writes with mid-century mandarin coolness and finesse about dogshit, dog sex, dog blood, dog passion, *dogs*, really getting down in dogginess—"doggery," he called it—while never losing his beautifully and ironically disso- nant fastidious/hilarious highbrow tone, is pretty much the last word in dog writing. In its day it was rather shocking. "Meaningless filth about a dog," pronounced Dame Edith Sitwell shortly after the book's publication in 1956.

Here's Tulip, a high-strung Alsatian, peeing: "In necessity she squats squarely and abruptly, right down on her shins, her hind legs forming a kind of dam against the stream that rushes out behind; her tail curves up like a scimitar; her expression is com- placent." Ackerley describes one of Tulip's shits as "a lavish affair," yells "Arseholes!" at a cyclist who is rude to her in the street, and watches fascinated as she goes into heat. "Her urine, in her present condition, appeared to provide her wooers with a most gratifying cordial, for they avidly lapped it up whenever she condescended to void it, which she frequently did. So heady was its effect that their jaws would at once start to drip and chatter together, not merely visibly but audibly."

Ackerley was a London literary man, editor of the BBC magazine *The Listener*, with a very active and racy homosexual life ("innumerable soldiers and sailors," as Peter Parker puts it in his very good biography), and I have to think it was all that specu-

lative prowling and cruising and sniffing about that
he did, all that devotion to the feral side of Eros,
that made him such a poet of the dog world. *My
Dog Tulip* is a very lightly, you could almost say
reluctantly, fictionalized account of his relationship with his real-life dog Queenie, to whom he
would apparently sing, on their walks together, a
homemade song:

> *Piddle piddle seal and sign,*
> *I'll smell your arse, you smell mine . . .*

Doggy doggerel, ha ha. Anyway . . . Around the
neighbourhood we go, me and Sonny and Sonny's
balls. And the other dogs seethe and shout, and the
squirrel upside-down on the tree trunk stares at us
in hateful fixity, etc., etc. Is Sonny an angel? By
no means. Off the leash he can be a total men-
ace. "Friendly?" asks the owner in the park, as her
drugged-with-domesticity dog comes bumbling
unsuspiciously towards us. "Uh, well I never really
know," I say. "Which I suppose means No . . ."
And then watch in dismay as Sonny launches himself savagely, teeth bared, at the startled animal.

Ball-driven behaviour, I suppose. Ball-manners.
Big dogs, little dogs, up-for-it scrappers and blame-
less cloudy-eyed seniors, he goes for them all. Or
he doesn't. Sometimes he makes a new friend,
instantaneously, inexplicably, and they fly in zany
euphoric circles. I truly never know.

More than once his balls have nearly got him killed. It was the aggression brewing in his balls, I must assume, that impelled him out of the park, on that narrowly nonfatal spring morning, to confront a dog on the other side of the street. That dog, for its own reasons, was wearing a muzzle—an unbearable provocation, apparently. So across the park went Sonny, clean through the psychic barrier of the little park entrance, and out into the road. I saw him do it, I saw my shouts going unheeded, I saw the car coming, I saw the great golden gears of the universe turning—not exactly in slow motion, but with terrible serenity.

The sound of impact was remarkable: a plasticky, irrevocable, cold-blooded, bad-news *crump*. And expensive-sounding, like a car hitting another car. "That's it," I thought. But no. Sonny, somehow, was unmaimed, unmarked, unbroken, OK. Mainly he looked embarrassed. Another time, on the same patch of road, he was rear-ended by a police cruiser, thumped in his hindquarters by the enormous bumper of the law—again harmlessly, although the look of weary disgust I got from the flat-nosed young cop at the wheel has stayed with me.

The other major consequence of my dog's ball-havingness is the *sniffing*. All dogs do a bit of sniffing, of course—Ackerley again: "Dogs read the world through their noses and write their history in urine"—but dogs with balls are over the top.

Sonny sniffs feverishly, indecently, engrossed to a disturbing degree in whatever it is he's smelling: a hydrant, a weed, a shoe, a bag, a patch of earth, some mystic gap of neglect now charged with desire. (Denise Levertov, in her wonderful doggy poem "The Rainwalkers," alludes to "the imploring soul of the trashbasket.") When he's sniffing he looks slightly insane or accelerated; he looks like an addict. Everything noble and contemplative in his nature seems to have been consumed. His head is lowered, moving snakily back and forth across the ground; his upper lip quivers in a wet half-sneer; his ribcage chugs; his body is humped and cur-like. He's *gone*: deaf to my imprecations ("Come on, Sonny! Fuck's SAKE!"), numb to the tugging leash. Massively irritating, if you're trying to get somewhere.

But then again . . . Am I going to stand here, all pissed off, swearing at my dog and telling him to hurry up? Or am I going to slow down, breathe, and try to accept this initiation into the sensorium of the dog world? The glistening leaf, the pulsing sphincter . . .

And am I going to accept myself as a fact in this dog world, no more or less complex than the other facts? Because that's the other aspect of all this, the other dimension: being *known* by a dog. Known as a thing in time, a thing in the day, a thing that munches vacantly on toast, and disappears to masturbate, and brightens when it has an idea, and winds itself up before a phone call, and emits a particular sniffing sound when it rises from a chair with the intention of taking you (the dog) for a walk, and then another sound when it changes its mind and sits back down . . .

"Dogs are geniuses of pattern recognition," a dog professional told the puppy-socialization class we attended—once—when Sonny was young. *Your* patterns, my God. The ones you're barely aware of. The secret liturgy of your day. And your volatilities too: the mood swings, shifts in muscular tension, etc. Your dog knows it all. As committed as you might be to the idea of your own fragmentedness, in your dog's loving eye it all adds up. You are a unified and very predictable being. Maybe. I wrote a poem about it. It's called "The Dog's Epitaph on his Master":

> You should have managed your moods, old
>   bastard.
> Your melancholia you should
>   have mastered.
> Sitting there blackly, stuck in a poem—
> If we never go out, how can we
>   come home?

So let us extract the lesson. Reality is not static, not fixed, not separate from us, not over there. If you're with a dog, and especially if your dog has his balls, you see—and are seen—doggily. And dog reality is nodding weeds and bleak ramps and gleaming incisors and shudderingly braking cop cars and *you*, standing there turning your head this way and that, being experienced on the dog level.

"Attention," writes the neurophilosopher Iain McGilchrist, "is not just another 'function' along-side other cognitive functions. Its ontological status is of something prior to functions and even to things. The kind of attention we bring to bear on the world changes the very nature of the world in which those 'functions' would be carried out, and in which those 'things' would exist. Attention changes *what kind of* a thing comes into being for us: in that way it changes the world."

So Sonny's balls have changed the world. Is that it? I think it is. Yes. It is.

ODE TO THE INEVITABLE

(Horace, *Book 2, Ode 14*)

Postumus old buddy, the years fly by, alack,
and you can be as good as you like, you won't
    hold back
the wrinkles, and the sag, and the weakness that
    makes you crawl
and rushing impossible death like a wave or a wall.

You can butcher three hundred bellowing bulls a
    day
on the altar of Pluto—nothing. No reply.
Gloomy god, he's consumed with underworld
    politics,
shackling up giants on the far side of the Styx.

Which, incidentally, we'll all be crossing,
princes and ploughmen, the sound and the
    unsound,
all of us currently taking up space above ground.
Did we make it through wars? Did we make it
    through mashing seas?
Do we sit on the porch with a blanket over our
    knees?

Well. How wailingly it winds, the river of grief,
hell-river, gall-black Cocytus, of sorrow the very
     spine.
And that's where we're going, my friend.
On the banks of that dark flood,
along with the doomed daughters of Danaus,
and Sisyphus rolling his boulder—
all the infernal celebrities—
you'll get yours and I'll get mine.

So it's goodbye to the huggable wife
and the livable house, and goodbye to your special
     trees,
the ones you cherished. Where you're headed,
the roads are lined with dim and detestable
     cypresses.

And your wines, Postumus, your beautiful fuming
     wines!
Laid down for the special occasion that never
     came,
they'll be sprung from your padlocked cellar, and
     guzzled and spilled
by him who comes after, your inheritor,
     what's-his-name.

ODE TO MY FLIP PHONE

Lump in my pocket, buzz in my thigh, beloved little ebony brick of a Kyocera flip phone, let me salute you.

I can't remember how long we've been together. Seven years? More? Even back then you were retro. The salesman in the phone store, I recall, spoke warmly of your indestructibility, as if that was your prime virtue: he said I could throw you against a wall if I wanted, and you'd just bounce off. But I would never do that.

Why can't I quit you? First, the obvious thing: you are not connected to the Internet. So for me you are a guardian of privacy. And by "privacy" I don't mean cookies or my Social Security number or whatever—I mean the precarious sphere of imagination in which I exist when I'm not diddling about online. I mean what's left of my nondigital self. The rags, the fishbones, the unconsumed parts—you protect them.

Second, you've become rather talismanic, socially. You stand for something. Perversity? Bloody-mindedness? Willed obsolescence? Sure, why not. It's like hanging around with a maladaptive friend: I enjoy watching people react to you. When I brandish you, flourish you, I get exclamations of pity and confusion. Especially from the young. "Look at you, man," somebody said to me the other day when I took you out to exchange numbers. "*Look* at you."

Your powers of distraction are limited. When I'm bored, or anxious, or angry, or bored-and-anxious-and-angry, I can't just pick you up and stare at you. Or rather, I can stare *at* you, but I can't stare *through* you. I can't gaze, slack-faced, into *there* . . . into that itchy, dreamy, eats-your-mind place. I'm stuck out here in the world with my boredom and my anxiety and my anger. I stand around, hands in my pockets. I feel the stinky breeze on my face. I hear the caged hum of the city, the caged hum of my brain.

Texting, with you, is a chore. I perspire sometimes, when I'm crunching your noisy little buttons: it sounds like I'm operating a telegraph. A decent sentence, with a couple of clauses, can take me five minutes. Anybody who gets a text from me knows I mean it.

At the bar, my friend Adam shook his head sadly: "I respect it, I really do. But they're going to make it so, so difficult for you." He's right. They'll get us in the end. They'll superannuate our love. One day, when we're trying to pay for something, or reserve something, or validate ourselves in some way, at a desk or at a counter, somewhere along the everyday tech frontier, we'll get knocked back, and that'll be that.

And on that day, sweet node of obstinacy, I'll have to step forward without you. I'll have to go on, into the complete and ultraconvenient dissolution of everything.

ODE TO RUSHING

Okay, white rabbit, what's it all about?

"Oh dear! Oh dear! I shall be late!" Alice is drowsing on the riverbank. Grass smell, dragon-fly sizzle, sweet torpors of summer. You rush past her, throbbing with rabbity haste. You pull a pocket-watch out of your waistcoat and frenziedly consult it. Then you disappear down a hole. Alice is amazed. She must follow you. She descends . . . into Wonderland.

Me, I'm always late. Or about to be late. Or working quite hard not to be late—barely overcoming lateness. What I mean is: I'm always *rushing*.

Oh dear! Oh dear! Why am I like this? I'm not leading anyone into Wonderland. On the contrary, I'm stuck on the surface, pinned down by the unmagical laws of time and motion. Squeezed horizons, clammy feet: these are the symptoms of a chronic belatedness. Somewhere someone is tut-tutting. So why do I do it?

There are theories. One: I'm a selfish bastard. Everybody must wait for me. Like a king, or a comet. Two: in a low-testosterone high-information twenty-first-century environment, a life neutered of genuine risk, this—rushing—is what passes for adventure. I should be hunting caribou. I should be tripping with the medicine man. Instead I create for myself these spurious little emergencies, and go palpitating around in a state of white rabbit-ness.

(There's something else too: a childish refusal to accept how long everything actually takes. How laden with time our lives are. I persist in believing, for example, in the face of all the evidence, that a shower takes five minutes. Washing, drying, dressing: the whole shebang. Five minutes. And drinking a cup of coffee, or tying my shoelaces, or typing that final sentence . . . These things, miraculously, take no time at all. They have no duration!)

Of course perfect punctuality doesn't really exist. It's an abstraction, a notional point on the continuum. To be on time, you have to be early—because if you're not early, you're late. And what does being early mean? It means padding your schedule, which is your life, with those loose minutes, those margins for error, those insulating layers of dead time. It means waiting rooms. It means the tickle of the abyss. I can't do it.

So I rush. It gives me momentum. Look at me. I'm swerving through crowds; I'm hurdling inter-ference. Thirty seconds means everything. Here I come. And if you're waiting for me, relax. Stop scowling. I'm never *that* late.

ODE TO THE UNEXPECTED REVERSAL

He was supposed to win. That was the point. He won everything.

To rewind somewhat: By 2016, as a fan, a viewer, a consciousness-on-a-couch, I'd drifted away from the Ultimate Fighting Championship, aged out of it maybe. Softer midriff, softer mind? Whatever, I'd lost touch. But he found me: Conor "The Notorious" McGregor. Peacocking around in his beautiful suits, lightly promising destruction to his enemies, he zapped through my culture filters.

Why? Because he won everything! Won it in style. McGregor, twenty-seven, a former plumber's apprentice from Dublin, was unbeaten, unbeatable, in the UFC. Him and being beaten, it seemed, were in different universes. His left fist was an astonishment.

On my laptop I watched, again and again, his 2013 fight against Max Holloway: There's McGregor, dazzling with witty hook kicks and punches from the future, and there's poor Holloway, the bruises slowly thickening his face in layers of bewilderment and sorrow. "Let's put him away," advises John Kavanagh, McGregor's coach and corner-man, icing him down between the second and third rounds. "More water?" "Yeah, a little bit," shrugs easy-breathing McGregor. He takes a sip. "I feel great." "You look beautiful," chuckles Kavanagh. "You look *beautiful*, man." I was in love.

The UFC was in love too. As the largest and most dynamic promotion in the still-emergent sport of Mixed Martial Arts (MMA), it needed stars. And McGregor was a star: the company's most bankable and resplendently entertaining character. Inside the Octagon, the eight-sided, chain-link-fenced UFC ring, he cut a figure of near-comic bellicos-ity, hoisting his fists and bending his knees like a Regency pugilist; outside of it he sold the fights like nobody else. He appeared on the March 2016 cover of *Fighters Only* magazine in a pink bow tie. He could talk, he could swagger: in his chewy Dublin accent he wound up, freaked out, and methodically maddened his opponents.

And he won and he won and he won. In Decem-ber 2015 he fought Jose Aldo for the UFC feather-weight belt, and the effects of the McGregor hype-out were startlingly visible: Aldo was a fear-some and seasoned fighter, but climbing into the Octagon he was skittish, cramped, out of focus. He was pre-beaten, and after thirteen seconds of bouncing, unbearable anxiety, he walked with what looked like relief into the good night of McGregor's left hand.

That's how I pitched it to my editors at *The Atlantic*: We have to write about this guy, we *have* to, because he wins everything. And they went for it. So in early March, with my MMA-practicing, UFC-literate friend John, I flew to Las Vegas to see McGregor fight, beat, Nate Diaz at UFC 196.

It was primary season in America, right between the eleventh and twelfth Republican debates, and as turbulence spanked the plane and the tray tables rattled, it occurred to me that we might have flown into a stray pocket of Trumpian oratory, Trump-breath, a little verbal chaos-cloud unmoored from its source and drifting hazardously at 32,000 feet. Hot air surrounded the fight, too—most of it McGregor's. "I'm certainly going to toy with the young boy," he said of Diaz (three years his senior) at the prefight press conferences. "I'm going to play with him." He ungallantly mocked Diaz for his work teaching jiu-jitsu to kids—"He makes gang signs with the right hand and animal balloons with the left hand!"—and then, more Tysonesquely, promised to eat Diaz's carcass in front of his "little gazelle friends." Diaz, rhetorically overmatched, sensibly confined himself to some villainous scowling and swearing.

You wouldn't have read about McGregor-Diaz—or about Holm-Tate, the equally sensational women's

MMA bout immediately beneath it on the bill at UFC 196—in the sports section of your Sunday paper. And yet there were 15,000 howling fans at the MGM Grand and some 1.5 million pay-per-view buys at $49.99 a pop or more. That was the UFC in 2016, as it is to this day: ubiquitous, but not fully visible, like tattoos or Lexapro.

What a long way it had come from its circus-of-violence origins. At the promotion's maiden event—UFC 1, in 1993—boxers fought grapplers, sumo guys fought karate wizards, and gorillas fought octopuses. All was mismatch, disproportion, and it was cartoonish and impure and very, very brutal.

Now the thing had been set in motion: people, fighters, maniacs began mixing it all up, and competition-level MMA entered a new phase. Blood flowed, unregulated. Joe Rogan, whose involvement with the UFC as commentator/interviewer dates back to 1997, has talked about the days when telling people you were professionally associated with MMA was like telling them you were in the porn industry. Slowly, out of the primordial blitzing and gouging, rules emerged. No head kicks to a downed opponent. No hair-pulling or groin strikes. Small padded gloves were introduced.

Today, every UFC event should by rights begin with a short, hats-off-please-gentlemen prayer of thanks to Blessed John McCain, who famously decried MMA as "human cockfighting" and whose senatorial intervention in the late '90s—when he persuaded thirty-six states to ban it from cable TV—obliged the UFC to clean up its act, thereby setting it on the road to mass appeal. Since the early 2000s, the sport has consciously counterbranded itself against the larger, less organized and slower-moving boxing industry: The UFC, with its near-monopoly on MMA, can crisply and dramatically give the fans the fights they want.

MMA today is a technical and highly evolved sport, and fans arriving at a UFC event have a coherent set of expectations. The mingling of the martial arts having multiplied the ways in which you can be rendered unconscious—by punch, kick, elbow jab, knee strike, or arm across the carotid artery (the "rear naked choke")—fighters generally proceed with great wariness. Of the three five-minute rounds in a standard MMA bout, two and a half can pass in a kind of supercharged inertia: the fighters bob and feint, each waiting for his opponent to commit himself, and beneath desultory cries of "Hit him!" you can hear the sizzle as force fields of tension collide and separate inside the Octagon.

For long stretches nothing happens. This is why an explosive, all-action knockout artist like McGregor was so valuable to the UFC. He *made* things happen.

The initial hype for UFC 196 was that McGregor was going up a weight class—from featherweight (145 pounds) to lightweight (155 pounds)—to fight the lightweight champion Rafael dos Anjos. If he beat dos Anjos, in other words (and for McGregor there was naturally no *if* about it), he would hold two belts and rule two divisions.

But dos Anjos broke his foot in training two weeks before the fight, and his last-minute replacement was Diaz, a brooding, slightly out-of-condition 170-pound welterweight from Stockton, California. So here was Conor McGregor, the fighting metrosexual, flamboyant flattener of dangerous little men, abruptly vaulting up two weight classes and chancing his reputation and his record on what was no longer even a title fight. Bang the gong of hubris! Hail the crazy volatility of the UFC!

Nate Diaz moved like a brawler inside a sensei inside a spider inside a teenager. His self-promotion, his self-branding, was minimal, almost inverted. Once in the Octagon, however, he would show a lively interest in heel-like behaviour: He liked to slap his opponents, drop his guard and taunt them, and flourish his middle finger in their faces. He cut easily and bled copiously. His jiujitsu was strong, as was his boxing. And for UFC 196 he played—beautifully—the scarred and skulking out-sider to McGregor's anointed champion.

The crowd that night in the MGM Grand was moody, bloodthirsty, intoxicated, tribal, diabolically fickle—which is to say, typical. A crowd from the dawn of time. And as McGregor's warm-up music, the spooky, wind-under-the-door croon of Sinéad O'Connor singing "The Foggy Dew" floated through the arena—*As down the glen one Easter morn / To a city fair rode I*—the Irishmen in the place filled their lungs and roared.

There he was, burrowing out of the tunnel with his entourage: buoyant, smiling, mantled in the tricolor of the Republic. He would make his millions. He would claim this victory for his people. He would freeze the gormless Diaz inside an enchanted sphere of whirling feet and stinging dandy's fists. And then he would drop him with that monster left.

Except he didn't. To get a sense of the predicament of Conor McGregor as the fight moved into its second round, take the following two quotes— "Reality was giving its lesson, its mishmash of scripture and physics" (Ted Hughes), and "Reality is that which, when you stop believing in it, doesn't go away" (Philip K. Dick)—and for the word *reality* substitute the words *Nate Diaz*. Predictably covered in blood, Diaz remained undevastated by McGregor's punching power, and quite unaffected by his charm— no foggy dew on *him*. Gristly, obdurate, irreducible, Diaz was still there.

McGregor, his whole game having coagulated around that huge repetitive left, was slowing down. Diaz was coming forward, heavily, to chants of "Di-*az*! Di-*az*!" from the now-turning crowd.

And he was landing shots. After some of them McGregor would nervously lick his lips, as if offended by the taste. Then a right-left combination dazed him, staggered him, and Diaz— fully himself at last—dropped his hands and gave McGregor a gory, gum-shield-distorted grin. The middle-finger-in-the-face was surely coming. McGregor went desperately for a takedown, scrambling to embrace Diaz's legs. It was a kind of surrender. Diaz, awkward customer turned nemesis, got on top of McGregor, straddled his back, swiftly and expertly worked an arm under his chin, and there ended the lesson: pride goeth before a rear naked choke.

INFAMOUS PUGILIST SUFFERS UNEXPECTED REVERSAL. Surely one of the best headlines ever, from the London *Independent*, 11 November 1996, the day after Mike Tyson's shock defeat at the hands of Evander Holyfield. McGregor-Diaz was not the only upset at UFC 196. The much-loved Holly Holm, defending her bantamweight belt in the women's division, was rear-naked-choked by Miesha Tate. (Although Holm, unlike McGregor, did not tap out as the choke sank in—she went to sleep punching, her fists groggily flailing the air until her brain cut the power.)

Two stars, dimmed or dented. Two brand ambassadors, horizontal. In the event's aftermath, as a backwash of depressed Irishry sloshed around the MGM Grand, the question arose: Had the UFC blown it, lost money, in its pursuit of the spectacular? Should it have taken better care of its champions, got them safer fights?

To which the only possible answer was: No way. Holly Holm, beautiful Holly Holm, literally went out swinging. The light in Nate Diaz's eyes as he reared up, wearing his upside-down crown of blood, from the prone and tapped-out form of Conor McGregor—it was miles away, worlds away. It was from *The Iliad*.

And we, the mob, had been confounded and refreshed. We were alive, alive, alive in a zig-zag universe. I could hear John on his cellphone to his girlfriend: "He lost! . . . Yeah! He *lost*!" The lights came up in the arena, and we all blinked and breathed and stared at each other like people released from a spell.

ODE TO PABLO NERUDA

The moon is a woman brushing her hair.
My heart, it clangs like a dropped guitar.
Kiss me, flower. Kiss me, peach.
Kiss me, poet with global reach.
Was your talent truly enormous
or is it just that Spanish is gorgeous?
In the end it doesn't matter.
We're fools for your Pablo Neruda patter.
And you had the gift: you knew how to express
the sense of organic happiness.
You made it the subject of many an ode—
happiness, kicking around in the road,
ore of the world, heat of the vein,
sturdy as bread and right as rain,
happiness, covered in bumblebee fur.
Big-spirited, indeed you were.

ODE TO BBQ CHIPS

There they are at the gas station mini-store: BBQ chips. Delicately bristling in their half-inflated bags. Rasping, one against another, in their pouches of trapped air.

Do you want to eat them? No, it's more frenzied than that, more chaotically oral—this appetite has the flavour of addiction. You want to possess them, to get the entirety of you around the entirety of them. You want them all at once, immediately, stuffed into your mouth and shattering gorgeously between your molars. You want to increase as they decrease. And then you want it all over again, until you feel ill.

You cannot consume them elegantly. There are noises, breathings, gushings of drool. Your mouth must open wide, dentist's-chair wide. At some point you're going to have to lick—or suck—your fingers, get that sticky, musky, orange-brown powder off them.

Is it possible that they want *you*? Between the desire and the object there is mutuality. Sometimes. Your body, or so it feels, needs that trashy salty-sweet fake BBQ nectar. And the voluptuousness of these chips cannot be realized, cannot be consummated, unless you gobble them down.

But there's no satiety with the BBQ chip, no natural limit. You want them, you want them, and then you never want to see them again. Nausea is their shadow companion, their black rider. Between the second and third paragraphs of this piece I ate half a five-ounce bag, and now my stomach is involved: it's shifting, rinsing, distending, bulging towards some kind of utterance, as if trying to have an actual *thought*. Don't they call it the second brain? What have I done to my second brain?

Their nutritional value is of course nil. Empty calories: what a beautiful phrase. No minerals, no vitamins, no virtues, as food, whatsoever. Rather Zen. Floating hoops of nullity, with the void shining through them. Maybe you should give them up—but then what? The craving will remain. The craving abides.

This is the sharp tooth of abstinence, isn't it, familiar to addicts of every degree. Remove the substance/bad habit/fun thing, remove the bag of BBQ chips, and what are you left with? A compulsion that suddenly has nowhere to go. So now it's flying around your body. Now it's seeping and spreading into your BBQ chip-less day.

And now you're obliged to deal with *that*.

ODE TO THE LEFT HAND

I raised the drumstick, brought it down, and a new world opened before me.

Not a nice new world. Not a shiny new world. This was a new world of dimness. Of weakness and tempo slump and failing emotional voltage. A world of getting it wrong. (Or—worse—getting it almost right, forever.)

I was sitting, at the time, at my practice drumkit, attempting one of the signature flourishes of the late John "Bonzo" Bonham, of Led Zeppelin: triplets with a left-hand lead. Do this properly, with the correct dosage of taste and power in each stroke, and you're a jazz-enabled thunder god. Half-ass it, fluff it, and you're a pair of old shoes tumbling down a plastic chute. You're a kicked-over bucket. When I lead with my right hand, my triplets are OK. Not Bonhamesque, not Bonzoid, but OK. But when I switch to the *left* . . .

Being human, reader, you know exactly what I'm talking about. Righty or lefty, you know that if you lead with your non-dominant hand, whether you're brushing your teeth or dismantling an unexploded bomb, then all the clichés of maladroitness will swarm upon you: the fists of ham, the fingers of butter, the multiplicity of thumbs. What one side of you can do quite well, the other side can barely do at all.

Why? What's it for, the weaker hand? Why this built-in asymmetry, this out-of-whack distribution of strength and fine motor skills? The biology of handedness is complex. I am by no means qualified to explain it. But the psychology, it seems to me, is pretty straightforward.

It goes like this: Inside your nervous system there lives a shadow person, a shadow you, shy and clumsy, dislocated, light-fearing, not nearly as good at things as you are. An underachiever, a nailbiter and a nosepicker, who would very much like to be left alone. And you can get in touch with this person, immediately and directly, by using your weaker hand. Very simple. Try and crack an egg with it, and there s/he is, there they are.

And to be non-dominant socially—we all know how that feels. Certain people do it to us. Bullies. Beauties. One's heroes. When I met Dave Grohl, for example, I was fathoms deep in the realm of the non-dominant.

Grohl is my drum hero. Dave Grohl, Dave Grohl, his prowess I extol. He's been my drum hero for the last thirty-five years, ever since I saw him playing in London with the Washington, D.C., punk band Scream. A vision: Nineteen years old, scrawny and bare-chested, faceless behind whippings of long bleached hair, playing not just hurtlingly and dynamically (and with multiple storms of cleanly articulated Bonzoid triplets) but with real *weight*, real consequence. No hesitation, no equivocation, every stroke a distinct event. There was almost a moral quality to it. His sense of *time* . . . It was as if he was tutoring us in the patterns of reality, its metre, the actual intervals between one thing and the next. I was awestruck.

Decades later I shake Grohl's hand, gush like a nit-wit and suffer a minor crisis of identity. Which is what's supposed to happen when you meet your heroes. They—at the moment of encounter—are bulging with superior light, and you are in your own shadow. The non-dominant holds you in its spongy grip.

Work the left say the sports coaches. Learn how to catch a ball, throw a punch, make a shot, with your weaker hand. Shouldn't the life coaches say it too? Talk to the left, engage the left, accept the left, enlist the left. By working with your gauche self, the muzzy and foot-dragging character who rises and sleeps with you, you're not even doubling your capacities—you're squaring them. Treat this charac-ter with a stern kindness, with a reproving warmth.

Maintain discipline. Insist on effort. Be patient. Be open: the left knows a thing or two, from sitting in the darkness all this time. Seek integration. Marvel, humbly, at just how frigging long it takes.

There's so much still to be brought out of yourself. The work of art. The improbable mission. The unprecedented friendship. The astonishing shift in perspective. They're lurking in left field, these possibilities. In the murk of the not-yet-tutored. In the cunning of the weaker hand.

ODE TO INSOMNIA

You have to get up.

That's the first thing. Don't just lie there and let it have its way with you. The sea of insomnia moves horizontally; over the little dike of your toes it comes, in a surge, washing along your body. Is someone lying next to you, dense with sleep, reproachfully unconscious? That's not helping either. So verticalize yourself. Escape the bed. Escape its maddening mammal warmth. Out you go, clammy-footed, into the midnight spaces. The bathroom. The kitchen. The abyss.

So now you're up. You've reclaimed a little dignity, a little agency. You're shaken, though. You make yourself a piece of toast; it pops up like a headstone. *Here lies all possibility of rest and refreshment.* Insomnia is no joke. Literally—the thoughts it produces are entirely and droningly humorless. Failure, guilt, money, sickness. On and on, blah blah. And over there, look, the world: the whole flawed and shuddering and horribly lit life-and-deathscape, with all of us shambling around the circuit like broken beetles. At 2:41 a.m., everyone who's awake turns into Hieronymus Bosch.

And therein, dear reader—my sleepless friend—lies the key: You're not alone. Even as you twist in these private coils, these very particular difficulties, you are joined with a mystical fellowship of insomniacs. You, we, are all out there, keeping an eye on things: a siblinghood, an immense and floating guild of piercingly conscious minds. What might happen, if not for our slightly agonized vigilance? Into what idiocies of optimism and vainglory might humanity collapse? We're like the Night's Watch in *Game of Thrones*, except there's red-eyed millions of us. Above the city rooftops it shimmers and flexes, it tingles over the snoozy suburbs: the matrix of our wakefulness.

"God time": that's what my late friend, the writer Gavin Hills, used to call insomnia. Meaning I think a release from the individual and partial, a release into the eternal. The clock goes weird in the small hours. It speeds up and it slows down. It has moods. You yourself have moods. Now the Gothic backchat of insomnia fills your mind with terrible news, terrible apprehensions; now you feel a strange peace. Now panic seizes you: how will you function in the morning, on so little sleep? You'll be grumpy, you'll feel ill, your brain won't work! You'll look like shit, too. What about that thing, meeting, conversation, procedure you're supposed to have?

And now you feel something else: an angelic compassion for your social, external self, for the buttressed and bashed-together you, so brittle, trying so hard, that you present to the world every morning. Maybe you think about the other bashed-together selves that you'll encounter, in the greyness of the day, and you feel compassion for them too. This is a pure gift of the small hours.

It's four a.m. You've experienced yourself, comprehensively. You've preserved the balance of global sanity. You've had pity on your fellow man. You have sniffed timelessness. Your work is done, insomniac.

Go back to bed.

ODE TO BEING DEAD

Far from the pressure of light,
    released from appetite,
safe under the hedge and beyond the heart's edge,
    out of the reach of bothering dreams,
they who raved recently now sleep decently in
      earth's long seams.

Surpassing all situations
    they rest at their final stations.
No duties claim them, no lawsuits name them,
    and nobody cares what they said.
I brush my teeth and think with relief of the
    sober and comfortable dead.

ODE TO MIDDLE AGE

From the outside it looks steady: it looks *resolved*. Sitting heavily, substantially, in a chair, with settled opinions and stodgy shoes—there's something unbudgeable about the middle-aged person. The young are volatile; the old are toppling into fragility. But the middle-aged hold their ground. There's even a kind of magnetism to it: this solidity, this dowdy poise, this impressive averageness. It looks complete.

But on the *inside* . . . You're in deep flux. A second puberty, almost. Inflammations, precarious accelerations. Dysmorphic shock in the bathroom mirror (a good cliché, a true one): Jesus, who *is* that? Strange new acts of grooming are suddenly necessary. Maybe you've survived a bout with something serious; you probably have a couple of fussy little private afflictions. You need that ointment, that liniment, that crumpled tube of whatever. It feels like a character flaw. Maybe it *is* a character flaw.

Meanwhile, Eros won't leave you alone, because that's what Eros is all about—not leaving you alone.

Fire in the bones; fire in the loins. Freshly searing, because your sexiness is going down the plughole. Vanity! Should you do the uninteresting thing and blow your life to pieces?

For all this, though, you are weirdly and unwontedly calm, like someone riding a bicycle without using their hands. You're not an apprentice adult anymore. You're through the disorientation period, the Talking Heads *How did I get here?* moment. You're through the angst and the panic attacks. You don't yet have the wild license of old age, when you can write gnarly scandalous poems like Frederick Seidel, or tell an interviewer—as the Who's Pete Townshend did—that it's "too late to give a fuck."

But you're more free. The stuff that used to obsess you, those grinding circular thoughts—they've worn themselves out. They've bored themselves to death. You know yourself quite well by now. Life has introduced you to your shadow; you've met your dark double, and with a bit of luck the two of you have made your accommodations. You know your friends. You love your friends, and you tell them.

A sense—at last—of having some things in common with the other humans, the other wobbling bipeds: this, too, is one of the gifts of middle age. Good experience, bad experience, doesn't matter: experience is what you share, the raw weight of it.

The crater around the eyes. The scratches upon the soul. The banging up against your own boundaries, your own limits.

Limits, limits, thank God for limits. Thank God for the things you cannot do, and that you *know* you cannot do. Thank God for the final limit: Death, who now gazes at you levelly from the foot of your bed, and with an ironical twinkle, because you still don't completely believe in him. Not completely. Not yet.

And it's not too late to change. They're still blowing their tops for you, the volcanoes of transformation. Can you be more yourself? Can you be less yourself? Can you live here, right here, in the middle of your years?

ODE TO NOT MEDITATING

I know, I know: it's good for you.

It's good for *us*, damn it. Good for the nation. You're not going to open your eyes after twenty minutes of meditation, sigh, rise slowly to your feet and then go charging off to sack the Capitol. Not immediately, anyway.

And I also know that a serious meditation practice is . . . serious. It's not about white blankets and gong sounds on your phone. It's not about smooth vibes. What you get, rather, when you start to meditate—when you first sit with yourself—is a rather stunning immersion in chaos: the whirling thoughts, the howling needs, the funky wiring, the sacked Capitols of your own nature. Light that stick of incense by all means, but it's the hell smoke of your personality that you'll be smelling.

I know all this, because I sat with myself (and sometimes with other people, also sitting with themselves) for a number of years. It helped me enormously. It calmed me down. I learned a lot.

But now I've stopped. And I have to tell you, I think I prefer myself as a non-meditator.

I stopped meditating during the pandemic, because . . . fuck it. With the world going flat as a pancake why should I care about levelling myself out? No steady drone of mental health for me, doctor. Give me the peaks. Give me the troughs. I bought myself a T-shirt that said *It's Not Drinking Alone If Your Cat Is With You* and worked my way fuzzily, one movie a night, a bottle of Jameson at my side, through the filmography of Jason Statham. (My cat has since died.)

Anyway, it's working for me. The practice of not meditating, as I have pursued it over the last couple of years—not meditating first thing in the morning, not meditating during the day, and taking particular care not to meditate in the evening— has brought me home. Sensations, nice and nasty, possess me. Emotions run me. I'm not observing my thoughts, as they arise one by one, unbidden, from the ever-bubbling bed of the brain; I'm *thinking* my thoughts. I'm not groping towards the white light of nothingness; I'm stewing in the somethingness. Am I a tad less tranquil? Uh, probably. But I like it.

Give it a shot, solemn sitter. Unwind your legs. Close your third eye and open the other two. Open them extra-wide. Shake hands again with the self. Your own brief and uniquely tangled self. You can always ride them again, those universal pulses, those glossy theta waves of deep meditation. They keep rolling; they roll forever. You, on the other hand, don't.

ODE TO THE NIGHT FOX

Is it right under your bedroom window?

Could be. Or it could be a half a mile away. This noise is unlocatable. It's the shriek of the city fox, shrilling and momentary. The night puckers around it. The houses freeze, the back gardens stop breathing.

Flat, no reverb. No sense of dimension. Just the shriek itself. And you can't call it *piercing*, because that implies trajectory—and this shriek has no start and no stop, seeming to have been snipped or sampled at random from a continuous otherworldly ribbon of fox-shriek.

But still, it enters you. A sound to wake the dead. Or if you're living, a sound to recall you to the basic terror, to the sharp end of having a mind. All comfort, all illusion sheared away. Just you in the cold world, the moon-colored world. As if you were created to hear this shriek.

There it is again.

And under your blankets you quake, exhilarated, at how far inside the outside has come.

ODE TO GETTING IT WRONG

December 2019, England: an evening soccer match.

Floodlit winter brilliance. Scintillating figures with dragon breath, some in yellow, some in blue. Norwich City are playing Tottenham Hotspur in the Premier League. Teemu Pukki, Norwich's fiercely scurrying Finnish striker, attracts a long, searching ball from Mario Vrancic onto the panels of his chest, bounces it down into his own path, and then, slicing between two Tottenham defenders, zeroes it past the scrambling goalkeeper and into the back of the net. Beautiful. Goal scorer wheels away in triumph, home crowd goes nuts, a pulse of sport-induced gladness lights up the grid.

But wait . . . Hang on. Oh Christ. Oh *fuck*. VAR. The Video Assisted Referee system, reviled innovation of the Premier League's 2019/2020 season, is "checking" the goal. A hundred miles away, at the VAR Hub in Stockwell Park, London, footage is being reviewed.

We're in limbo. The announcers don't know what to say; the crowd shifts, grumbles, in a haze of spoiling endorphins. Then, on the big screen, there it is: GOAL DISALLOWED. A haggard roar goes up.

It has been determined that Pukki, at the moment that Vrancic sent the ball his way, was minutely, microscopically—with perhaps the outer edge of his shoulder—ahead of the deepest-lying Spurs defender: in other words, he was offside. The referee didn't see it; the linesmen didn't see it; the crowd didn't see it; the Tottenham players didn't see it. Nobody saw it. But the faceless invigilators of VAR, in their multiscreen hive—they saw it. Sorry, Pukki. Sorry, universe. Wind back the spool of joy. No goal.

Watching VAR happen, watching this huge, technocratic toad lower its clumsy haunches onto the game of soccer, I feel ill. I feel, as William James put it, menaced and negated in the innermost springs of my life. Why am I so upset?

Well, I'm aesthetically disgusted, first of all. Soccer is a drama and a spectacle: VAR is anti-dramatic, anti-spectacular. We are obliged to wait while some people, somewhere else, appraise some data. Fantastically unexciting. Anti-rhythmical, too: it puts a great glitch of second-guessing into the flow of the game.

Second, my soul rebels. The deep-space pedantry of VAR, the VAR-world with its obscure vectors and subatomic infringements, seems to me literally inhuman. How are we, flawed beings with holes in our trousers, supposed to survive under these levels of supervision, this overweening scrutiny?

So, here's to being fallible: to honouring the possibilities of the ever-running moment by accepting that some of those possibilities are *wrong*. Perfectibility, in life as in soccer, is a malign fantasy: it does a lot of damage. A tolerance for error is a must. Not for injustice, not for corruption, but for the honest mistake, made in real time.

Solomon himself blew a call now and again. So what? It's a universal condition. It's *the* universal condition. You don't hit "Pause" and summon the tech priests. You don't wait for the screen to tell you what happened. You don't stop the game until the game is over.

ODE TO CONSTIPATION

My cat sticks his head
round the bathroom door
and regards me
with small humorless cat-face.

ODE TO THE EVERYTHING
THAT ISN'T ME

Beautiful world-altering things, when they enter history, when they enter time, it kind of happens off to one side. The cameras are always pointing in the other direction. The crowd is always looking the wrong way. So it was with the birth of Jesus. So it was with the sound of AC/DC.

It's the mid-1970s. The nearly punk rockers, the pre-punks and the proto-punks and the conceptualists and the journalists and the punky poets, are all fuming and scheming and swapping mad stares. It's about to happen. They can already hear it: a stripped-down rock'n'roll noise that will kill all the hippies forever. A pure assault, a quintessence, beyond which no further refinement is possible. They can taste it. They can almost, almost, with their instruments and their voices, *make* it. But not quite.

So where does it come punching through, this sound? Out of the realm of perpetual possibility and into our tatty old world? Not in the teeming punk rock ratholes of London or New York, and not in the arty lofts either. It happens in Sydney, Australia. Courtesy of two tiny Scotsmen.

By 1975, the band built by Malcolm Young and his little brother Angus was already the complete statement: sawn-off Chuck Berry riffs, blood-throb bass, stripped-to-the-essentials 4/4 drums and boisterously antisocial lyrics, everything delivered with a special edge of mania. Their only technology was amplification (and just a *bite* of distortion on the guitars). It was all in the finest sense reactionary, which meant that nothing like it had been heard before.

They weren't punk rockers. They didn't snipe or thrash or clatter. This sound was huge-boned, blues-rooted. And performed with throttle-your-guitar-neck grip and professionalism. Nonetheless, it's a fact: at the dawn of punk rock, year zero, the planet's fiercest destroyer/creators were AC/DC.

Scowling Malcolm (5′ 3″), chop-chopping out the chords on his Gretsch with a skinny arm, was a player of pulverizing succinctness. In another life he might have been an extraordinary lead guitarist. But in the primordial division of powers at the birth of AC/DC it was determined that he should play rhythm. So Malcolm became the master of negative space, god of the gaps, conjuring those riffs out of an enormous energized silence. The lack of distortion in his tone—the low gain on his amp, the lack of *metal*—guaranteed that every coiled under-chord, every checked backstroke, every tucked-in absence was heard and felt. "Highway To Hell": the spaces ring out. His riffs, his mega-riffs, are all about what isn't there. Malcolm ruled the vacuum.

Which meant that Angus (5' 2") could do the opposite thing. Angus, playing lead guitar, became the note-spewer, the galactic decorator. He poured substance; he streamed with essence. Contrast their onstage presences. Malcolm, tiny titan, twitched grimly and rootedly as he played, as if the earth beneath his feet was delivering continual small shocks. But Angus, dressed in his school uniform, was on the move. He was all over the place. He was a duckwalker and a headbanger—possibly the first headbanger.

Here's the vision of Angus playing: the little rubbery legs go bounce-bounce with the left knee, bounce-bounce with right, and between the goblin wingstumps of his sticking-out elbows the handsome outsized head—mouth open, eyes closed—flails slowly up and down over the red Gibson. He is nodding, he is saying Yes. Life: he agrees to it. The right arm lifts, rises, in an absent-minded salute, as the fingers of the left hand bend and compel the strings. Ssssh. Angus is CONCENTRATING.

The brothers, the guitars. Malcolm's sound was not the dense and unstoppable heavy metal power chord, going on forever: it had breath in it, finitude, a shining perishability. And in Angus's playing, in his fingering, you could hear *bagpipes*. Seriously. A windblown wistful Celticism. Play the intro to "Thunderstruck" and there it is, threading through the euphoria—the wheedling, pealing plaint of the bloody bagpipes.

They had a rhythm section. What a rhythm section: Phil Rudd on drums, playing with a disco-pistoned savagery that none of the punk bands (or even the post-punk bands) could hope to match, and Cliff Williams, architect of those thrumming, pummelling, funnelling, tunnelling, monomaniac, steady-state eighth-note basslines—*bum-bum-bum-bum-bum-bum-bum-bum*—conductor of a tension that he would finally release, with not an erg of energy lost or thrust mislaid, into the grand plunge of the chorus.

And they had a singer. What a singer: Bon Scott, shirtless tattooed brawler, snaggle grin, working-class Dionysus, with a unique quasi-flamenco wail that he maintained, according to legend, by gargling port before shows. Hard nut, soft heart. The chemistry was perfect. Listen to "Shot Down In Flames": "Hey you!" shrieks Bon just before the two-minute mark. "Angus! *Shoot* me!" Cue a series of rocketing pick-slide *glissandi* from his lead guitarist, shearing their way between Malcolm's monster chords. "That's NICE!" declares Bon, and continues to frazzle in lowbrow ecstasy— "Uh! Oh! Wooh!"— through a typically witty and idea-packed flight from

Angus. When Jimmy Page soloed, Robert Plant would arc his back and whoop like Maid Marian having her bottom pinched; Pete Townshend could force a sort of orgasmic bluster from Roger Daltrey; David Bowie theatrically fellated Mick Ronson's fretboard; but Angus really *tickled* Bon Scott.

And because they were perfect, the universe gave them the perfect producer: Robert John "Mutt" Lange. The only man who could make AC/DC more AC/DC than they already were.

What is the Mutt Lange AC/DC sound? A miraculous fertile dryness, a compression that is paradoxically expansive. A kickdrum that seems to create its own pocket of spacetime. Multi-multi-multi-tracked guitars, panned hard in the left and right channels for a thicker, more 3-D effect. (As Jesse Fink writes in *The Youngs*: "You can *see* the music.") Great size, great detail, like mountains in clear light. That strange, beery choir, triumphally decelerated, yelling "Highway tuh *HELL!*" . . . Malcom's gaps, his magnifying lulls, moving like shockwaves across this new zone . . . Mutt Lange gave AC/DC *scale*. And then— hits. With *Highway to Hell*, the first of three Mutt Lange–produced albums, AC/DC broke America.

Now comes the tragic hiccup in the AC/DC story. London, 1980: after a night of kamikaze boozing, alone and covered in a blanket in the back of a parked Renault 5, Bon Scott succumbs. His band-

mates are privately shattered; the entity called AC/
DC, however, coughs once, shakes its head and
carries on. Within a month of Scott's death audi-
tions are being held in a cold London rehearsal stu-
dio. Posers, no-hopers, prima donnas, and genuine
prospects go flickering across the band's viewfinder.
Who can follow Bon? Enter Brian Johnson, from
the north of England, in a flat cap.

Johnson, in the best possible way, is post-AC/DC:
his voice—shrill, ragged, spinal—is reactive. It
records, at a constant peak, the almost-superhuman
excitement of being in AC/DC, of finding oneself
fronting this band. Onstage his authority is Scott-
level, and as a writer he started strong (*Knockin' me
out with those American thighs,* one of the great AC/
DC lines, is his), but over the long haul it must be
admitted that, lyrically, there has been something
of a falling-off.

Musically, however, the compound admits of no
adulteration. One cannot be influenced by AC/
DC—one can only rip them off. AC/DC rip themselves off all the time. Like Motörhead and the
Ramones, their worst productions tend to mechan-
ically travesty their best.

By the time I finally saw them, at the Gillette Sta-
dium, home of the New England Patriots, it was
2015. A rough season for AC/DC: The previous

year it had been announced that Malcolm Young, sixty-two, was suffering from dementia and could no longer continue in the band. (Grotesque irony, that Malcolm, author of the most unforgettable riffs in rock and roll, should now be unable to remember them.) Then Phil Rudd was arrested and later convicted of drug possession and threatening to kill a former employee. Chris Slade was now on the drums, while Malcolm's slot was filled by his fifty-eight-year-old nephew, Stevie.

So we were far, here, very far, from the band's hooligan pomp. Now—more interestingly perhaps, and certainly more movingly—we were bearing witness to its wild senescence. Dusk fell and the air cooled, and the great bowl of the Gillette scintillated with the restless, insectile blink-blink of a thousand pairs of toy devil horns—tiny red lights, everywhere. (You could get your horns at the concession stand, all part of AC/DC's jolly postmodern diabolism: "Hell Ain't a Bad Place to Be.") And there on the big screen was Angus, with his pale, bare shins and his gibbering kneecaps and his head going up and down, up and down, in a contemplative frenzy, a sixty-year-old man dressed like a schoolboy. He struck his black Gibson, right arm lifting away from it in weightless tribute. It took a second for the sound to reach us, and in that time lag was the span of our adoration. *AN-GUS! AN-GUS!*

Why, in my life, has the music of AC/DC been such a tonic, banisher of depressions, holy resource? I depend upon it. From holes it can pull me, from cellular sulks it can rouse and redeem me, and from the most maggoty fit of sloth. I'm not alone in this. Hundreds of thousands of people dose themselves similarly with the music of AC/DC. For a boost, for a buzz. For salvation.

Why? Because it's a shaft of the Absolute, attracted earthward and split into guitars/drums/voice by some vulgar and canny Australians. Because it shatters solipsism and makes sunkenness-in-the-Self impossible. Because, in its bountiful joyful crass rock'n'roll immensity, it's the face of the everything that isn't me.

ODE TO SMALL TALK

The correct answer to the question "How are you?" is *Not too bad*.

Why? Because it's all-purpose. Whatever the circumstances, whatever the conditions, *Not too bad* will get you through. In good times it expresses a decent pessimism, an Eeyore-ish suspicion of getting carried away. On an average day it's got a nice, muddling-through modesty to it. And when things are rough, really rough, it becomes a heroic understatement. *Not too bad* was especially useful during the pandemic: those three equally stressed syllables could be heard clearly through the mufflingest, most bafflingly layered mask. How are you doing, fellow blunderer through this world-historical germ cloud? How *are* you? *Not. Too. Bad.*

Small talk is rhetoric too. Americans in particular are small-talk artists. They have to be. This is a wild country. The fibers attaching one person to the next, the fibers of consensus and cooperation, are very, very tenuous. So the Have-a-nice-days, the Hot-enough-for-yous, the How-'bout-those-Celticses—extremely important. Without them, without these emollient little going-nowhere phrases and the momentary social contract that they represent, there'd be shooting in the streets. Which is to say, more shooting in the streets. Small talk: our last bastion against American carnage.

But that's to take the negative view. Some of my most radiant interactions with other human beings have been fleeting, glancing moments of small talk. It's an extraordinary thing. A person stands before you, unknown, a complete stranger—and the merest everyday speech-morsel can tip you headfirst into the blazing void of his/her soul.

(Not everybody wants their talk small, of course. Crossing Boston Common in the winter of 2018 I spotted a man I know—a writer who at that time was homeless. Delighted to see him, I rushed over. "Ken!" I said. "How's life?" He looked at me with real disappointment: "How's *life*?! . . . I thought we were going to have a nice conversation.")

I was out walking the other day when a UPS truck rumbled massively and fudge-brownie-ishly to the curb in front of me. As the driver—shorts, mighty tanned calves—leaped from his cab to make a delivery I heard music coming out of the truck's speakers: a familiar, weightless strain of blues-rock noodle. Could I identify it? That special spacey twinkle in the upper registers, that special flimsiness in the rhythm section . . . Yes. It had to be.

The Grateful motherfucking Dead, in one of their zillion far-from-essential live recordings. And I knew the song, because it's my favourite Dead song. "China Cat Sunflower?" I said to the UPS guy as he stormed back to his truck. A huge grin: "You got it, babe!"

The exchange of energy, the perfect understanding, the freemasonry of Deadhead-ness that flashed instantaneously between us, and most of all the honorific *babe*—I was high as a kite for the next ten minutes, projected skywards on a dazzling beam of small talk.

ODE TO BAD REVIEWS

Should writers respond to their critics? No, no, a thousand times no.

A writer should never respond to his or her critics. A writer should rise above, shimmer clear, in wonderful aloofness.

Sometimes that's not possible, of course. I was drinking with a friend in London when he spotted, on the other side of the bar, a man who days before had reviewed him cruelly in a national newspaper. My friend grew agitated. "I'll punch him in the face!" he said. "No, wait. I'll buy him a drink!" He paused. "What should I do?" He had no idea, and neither did I. Aggression, under the circumstances, seemed quite as promising/futile as magnanimity. I don't even remember what he did in the end. The point is: you can't win.

"Sometimes you are the pigeon," Claude Chabrol said, "and sometimes you are the statue." Wise, cigarette-smelling words. But we are not statues—we are not made of stone. Shat upon, do we not feel it? And right now everybody feels it.

Getting a bad review is no longer an elite experience. Writers and non-writers, mandarins and proles, we've all been trolled, orced, goblined, Black Ridered in some thread somewhere, at the bottom of some page.

Scroll down, scroll down, take that Orphic trip into the underworld of the comments section, and there they are—the people who really object to you. Their indignation, their vituperation, is astonishing. It seems to predate you somehow, as if they have known and despised you in several former existences. You read their words and feel undone. Get out of this place immediately. Run toward the light. Let the dead bury their dead. And don't look back—because if you do, like Orpheus, you'll lose what you love the most.

Also, sometimes they're right! In his memoir *Prince Charming* the great poet Christopher Logue, in mellow old age, dives into "a chocolate-liqueur box filled with dated clippings of every review that my books, plays or radio programs had received since 1953." He makes a discovery. "How differently they read now. At the time, oh, the complaining: That fellow failed to praise me for this, this fellow blamed me for that. . . . Now, how fair-minded their words appeared, how sensible their suggestions for my improvement." I know what he's talking about here. A piece I once wrote for *Slate* elicited the following comment from a reader:

"Fragile conceit held together by disintegrating threads of fancy." Which stung at the time, but is actually a pretty good description of . . . me.

But there remains that feeling of being misunderstood and misused. That subtracted, sad-child feeling. You may be wondering how it is that I, who have written derisively and destructively about things I considered not good, who have taken pains to make public, in as amusing a way as possible, the inferior qualities of this or that artist, can be so terribly thin-skinned. Is it the case, you ask shrewdly, that I can dish it out but can't take it? To which I reply: It is absolutely the case. I can dish it out endlessly, and I can't take it at all. In other words, I'm just like you.

I'm learning, though. We're all learning. We're all getting a little more sensitive. So, to the authors I have injured with my criticism, I say this: Your book may not have improved, but my moral qualities have, very slightly, and I regret the pain I caused you. And if we happen to meet one day, punch me in the face and buy me a drink.

ODE TO SEIZING THE DAY

(Horace, *Book 1, Ode 11*)

Don't peer ahead. Don't pluck the web of Time.
How long we've got, the loving gods won't tell
and your Babylonian horoscopes have no clue.
Acceptance. That's the trick to living well.
This could be our last winter, watching the waves
pound themselves silly on the Etruscan shore . . .
Season your expectations; rack your wine
and filter out the crap. Don't be a bore.
While we've been talking, ten minutes flew away.
Just do it. Gather ye rosebuds. Seize the day.

('Twas I, Quintus Horatius Flaccus, who coined
that cliché.)

ODE TO SQUIRRELS

Why are you squawking at me, little messenger?

Why are you up in that tree, clenched, flickering your tail in a fury and showering me with pissed-off noises? What have I done to upset you?

Well, I think I know. You're vexed by my dull-ness. My denseness. You see me lumping along the sidewalk, with my five sleepy senses and a private *Truman Show* raincloud over my head, and you're outraged. You can see that I'm getting about 2 percent of what's going on. So you yell at me, in croaks and leathery quacks: *Wake up!*

Not that I'd want what you've got. Too intense. Being a squirrel, having squirrel-ness? No thanks. I've seen you doing your pouncing runs and your sudden stops. It's like you're in the last scatty spirals of a drug binge. Threats, it seems, are everywhere. You rush, you rush, and then you freeze—you wait, breathless—and the whole scene around you sort of *wobbles*, caught in the blast radius of your vigilance. Then you rush again. It's exhausting.

Who lives closer to us, in the city, than you do? The pigeon is of the air, and the rat hides his face. But you are everywhere, sharing our daylight spaces, offering your weird nibbling commentary. And just because you're paranoid, tiny gargoyle, doesn't mean that they're not after you. From time to time I find you dead, super-dead, extravagantly terminated: flattened or charred or sliced in half. My dog is a threat, a real one. He'd kill you if he could. But he never can. You dodge him always, corkscrewing around a tree trunk or dancing ninja-like along a fence. His reality is sharper than mine, and yours is sharper than his.

This is why I appreciate you, squirrel—why I peer into treetops and scan the rubbishy park for your withered little unblinking face. I love the wildness with which you accompany my unwildness, the many spikes of terror and appetite that pierce your soul while I'm wondering if I left the car unlocked.

Is it your world, or is it mine? Is this a quiet grey street, my street, or the set of a feral opera? There you go, tree-leaping again, off on some desperate journey. The branches nod gravely as you race across them.

ODE TO NAPS

With the nap it can go either way.

It can work—which is to say it can perform its function of refreshment and revival. Twenty minutes or so of light untroubled sleep, just when you need it. After lunch, perhaps. Nature herself gently makes the suggestion. Close your eyes, she offers, and digest.

So you settle, you sink. But not too far. A delicious shallowness. You open your eyes: you're awake again. In a state of lamb-like innocence, blinking limpidly and contentedly, pleasantly energized. The prickle of health is on your skin. Ah, it feels so good. What a great idea that was, to take a nap.

Or it can . . . not work. You go down, you get swallowed. Sweatings, fidgets, moaning. After a slow-motion, deep-sea struggle, you haul yourself awake. You're back, sort of. But you've spent too long in the coils of Morpheus; now his chemicals are in your blood. You've aged, visibly. Your face looks like a sat-on bagel. Your last five meals are burning black smoke in your system. You blunder into the kitchen, craving sugar. The afternoon ahead of you is grey with difficulty. Taking a nap was the worst idea in the world.

And you never know, that's the thing. Certain life variables may apply—your hormones, your glands, your booze intake, your bank balance—but basically it's a mystery. The good nap alights upon you like the grace of God: weightless, unmerited, spirit-altering. The bad nap, the sad nap, lies in wait like Wile E. Coyote with an anvil.

Sleep experts will tell that an afternoon nap interferes with what Bertie Wooster called "my usual nine hours of the dreamless." It jangles the bio-rhythms, they say, and buggers up the brainwaves. But what do they know? We are living in a special time. All data pre-2016 is moot. The sleep studies: start them over. We're different animals now.

I say go for it. If there's a space for zzzzs in your day, if you glimpse a passing snooze-pocket, jump into it, by God. Mix yourself with insensibility wherever it presents itself. Do it for all of us, for the balance of dark and light, because there's too much consciousness around right now, too much alertness, too much anguished attention. Shut off, shut down. Sleep is merciful. Sleep might help. Seize the nap.

ODE TO MY THESAURUS

They've got you all wrong.

They think you're a trick, a cheat sheet for fancy words, a way of counterfeiting cleverness. (And Americans are fatally awed by cleverness. This new drama/author/tweet/whatever is always "whipsmart." That drunk guy is always shouting *Think you're smarter than me? HUH?*)

Or they'll treat you as a mere lexical resource. A vocabulary-expander. A thighmaster for out-of-condition prose. I mean we've all done it. Reached for you, that is, when the words arriving at our forebrain, from the tatty little glossary that we keep in our backbrain, seem . . . insufficient. Don't say *in a shitty mood*. Say *captious*.

But that's not how, or when, to use you. That's not who you are. You, my friend, are a vision. You're a shamanic trip into the essence of words: a shimmering, unfolding, occasionally scarifying million-petalled kind of an experience, a miraculous nest of emergent relationships, and the writer who abuses your nature, who exploits your abundance, will pay. He will pick the wrong word, and he won't sound clever at all. He'll sound like an ass. He'll sound like a *silly-billy, twerp, stooge.*

Here's what you're for, thesaurus: you're for increasing our aliveness to words. Nothing more and nothing less. By going into the buzzing and jostling hive of words *around* a word, we get a purer sense of the word itself: its colouration, its interior, its traces of meaning. I looked up the verb *excite* just now and found the word in its affective (*touch, move*) and mechanical aspects: *electrify, galvanize.* Which gets at who we are, as humans, doesn't it? Feelings and circuitry.

Lewis Carroll made up *chortle*, and you absorbed it, placing it snugly between *chuckle* (benign and big-bellied) and *cackle* (witchy and weird). Ken Dodd, the great English comedian, made up *tattifilarious.* "Now," he told an interviewer as an old man, "now is reality. And it's wonderful. By Jove, it's tattifilarious!" You have not, as yet, absorbed that. I'd float it in there somewhere between *bittersweet* and *custard-pie.*

As for you, blessed Mr. Roget, they say you had OCD. Of course you did. You were *hooked on, hung up, haunted by* the hidden life of words: their selves, their stories, as told by the words they are closest to. You gave us a great gift. May you rest eternally among your synonyms.

ODE TO PURGATORY

Increasingly, I find,
it sits upon my mind.

My dog licks my forearm in his earnest
   doggy fashion,
and I think of cleansing tongues of
   purgatorial fire,
lapping at my soul with a passion.
Someone leaves me a voicemail.
I ignore it because I'm not in the mood.
And I think: you'll be listening to that one
in Purgatory, dude.

The things overlooked, the
   things undercooked,
the things neglected and uninspected . . .
The people with whom we were careless
   or feckless,
the people with whom we got bored—
they're waiting for us in Purgatory,
a quivering zombie horde.

Life is largely getting away with it.
But Purgatory is where you spend all night
    and all day with it.
Everything counts in large amounts, sang Dave
    Gahan of Depeche Mode.
And there I end my ode.

ODE TO RUNNING IN MOVIES

Dash into the flames. Fling yourself at the spiky green shins of the monster. Outpace the avalanche, or come windmilling, wide-mouthed, out of the collapsing ice palace. Running in movies is always towards danger or away from it. No one in movies is ever just *running*.

And like ballet dancers, the great runners-in-movies express character through movement, through the whirling and thumping of their limbs. Matt Damon, as Jason Bourne, is a brain-wiped super-soldier having an identity crisis, so he runs like a frightened washing machine. Carrie-Anne Moss, as Trinity in *The Matrix*, runs like an enigma from the future—which is what she is. Harrison Ford in his prime had a distinctive bowled-over running style: look at him in *The Fugitive*, blundering and floundering and grimacing and reeling, an everyman dislodged from the everyday, blown out of his life, and frowningly, headbuttingly determined to get back in there.

(Tom Cruise is different: whatever part he's playing, Jerry McGuire or Jack Reacher, he runs like

Tom Cruise, with piston knees and piston elbows and the face of an angry Christ. And that's OK.)

Bradley Cooper in *Silver Linings Playbook*, pounding and perspiring around the 'burbs with a garbage bag sort of medievally layered over his hoodie, is jogging. People do jog in movies, for fitness—but *interiorly*, as they jog along, they're still firmly located on that into-trouble/out-of-trouble axis. They're still going one way or the other. Cooper is running for his sanity. He's running—so he hopes—out of madness.

We are especially close to the joggers-in-movies, perhaps because jogging is something *we* can do. We can each of us, bodies allowing, dramatize our personal arc of character with a bit of jogging. Huff, puff, yes I'm getting *fitter* . . . But I'm over jogging. It's extremely boring, for a start. And also, I think, of dubious moral value. The lone, twanging jogger, with his privately pulsing heart and his tiny private agenda of self-betterment: that's so pre-pandemic. The other thing is, I'm in my fifties, and my knees hurt.

So give it up, I say. Let the couch exhale, like a prizefighter taking one to the kidneys, as you land heavily upon it. Sit back, and glory in the varying styles of the great runners-in-movies. It could be Franka Potente (*Run Lola Run*); it could be Cobie Smulders (*Results*); it could be Rocky, shlepping with wracked breath up the steps of the Philadelphia Museum of Art.

For me it's got to be Daniel Day-Lewis as Hawkeye in *The Last of the Mohicans*.

If you've seen the movie, he's in your head right now—a swooping, swerving, low-shouldered, soft-footed runner, moving through the woods, moving through his element. His face is a mask of focus; he seems to use no peripheral vision; sometimes he has a loaded musket in each hand; an enemy rears up, he drops him without pausing, and he doesn't look back.

ODE TO COLD SHOWERS

Here's what used to happen.

I'd wake up, smouldering and sighing, reel out of bed and into the kitchen, and put the kettle on. Then I'd think: well, now what? Time would go granular, just particles of stuff, like in a Jack Reacher novel. But less exciting. Five minutes at least until the kettle boils. Make a decision. Crack the laptop, read the news. Or stare murkily out the window. Unload the dishwasher? Oh dear. Is this life, this sour weight, this baggage of consciousness? Is this me? What's that smell? It's rising fumes of futility. At seven a.m.

Here's what happens now.

I wake up, smouldering and sighing, reel out of bed and into the kitchen, and put the kettle on. And then I have a cold shower.

I don't want to go overboard here, reader. Life-changing, neurosis-cancelling, enlightenment at the twist of a tap—I don't want to make these claims for the early morning cold shower.

But if, like me, you have a sluggish seam of depression in your nature, and a somewhat cramped brain, and a powerful need, throughout the day, for quasi-electrical interventions of one sort or another, reboots and renewals—or if you just want to wake up a little faster—can I most devoutly recommend that you give it a shot?

Do it first thing. Soon as you get up. Put the kettle on, and then: straight at it. Don't torture yourself with postponement. And don't muck around—unless you have to—with hot-to-cold transitions, temperature tweakings, etc. Fling wide the plastic curtain, crank the tap to its coldest, take a breath and step right in. Not grimly or penitentially, but with slapstick defiance: *Holy Mother of God! Cowabunga! Here I go!* (If it's too early in the day for slapstick defiance, try a headshake of weary amazement.)

The water hits, and biology asserts itself. You are not a tired balloon of cerebral activity; you are a body, and you are being challenged. You gulp air; your pulse thumps. Your brain, meanwhile, your lovely furry old brain, goes glacier-blue with shock. Thought is abolished. Personality is abolished. You're a nameless mammal under a ravening jet of cold water.

It's a species of accelerated mindfulness, really: in two seconds, you're at the sweet spot between nonentity and total presence. It's the cold behind the cold, the beautiful immobile zero, a flame of numbness bending you to its will. Also—this is important—you can get all your washing done in a cold shower: hair, body, everything. The coldness is no obstacle to a good lathering-up.

Then you get out, and you're different. Things have happened to your neurotransmitters that may be associated, say the scientists, with *elevated mood* and *increased alertness*. You're wide awake, at any rate. Your epidermis is cool and seal-like. Your nervous system is jangling—but melodically, like tiny bells. And from the kitchen, you can hear the kettle starting to whistle.

ODE TO ELECTRICITY

It's pretty straightforward. All art aspires to the condition of music, and all music aspires to the condition of Jimi Hendrix.

Plucked out of New York City by manager/impresario Chas Chandler, Hendrix arrives in London in September 1966: Lone guitarist, lanky acid popinjay, sci-fi African American with Irish-Cherokee blood. His manners are almost courtly, his speech a singsong sequence of half-groans, groovy hesitations, delicate chuckles, fond suggestions, and trailing colors, a kind of elasticized stammer. His physical presence is dramatic but somehow only partially materialized—at his edges he seemed to blur into fumes, mental incense.

Who is this person? He's a liability, first of all. A shy boy who is also a semi-deranged showman. Druggy, unmanageable, twenty-four years old, he's already had a brief career drifting around under parachutes in the 101st Airborne ("I believe the military service will benefit if he is discharged as soon as possible," was the considered verdict of his platoon sergeant) and several even briefer careers playing guitar for the Isley Brothers, Little Richard, Curtis Knight, and whoever else on the R&B circuit would hire him (and then fire him). Writes Philip Norman in the Hendrix biography *Wild Thing*: "Curtis Mayfield expelled him for accidentally damaging an amplifier. On tour with Bobby Womack, his behavior was so exasperating that Womack's road-manager brother threw his guitar out of the bus window while he was asleep."

Additionally, he's a genius. Billy Cox, when he first heard Hendrix's playing, through the door of an army club, imagined a mingling of John Lee Hooker and Beethoven. Chas Chandler, Englishman in New York, watches him do "Hey Joe" at the Cafe Wha? and hears a hit. Hendrix is going to London.

Chandler procures him a rhythm section. Two Brits: Noel Redding on bass, Mitch Mitchell on drums. Is this a musical mismatch, pasty Limeys dragging down the Dionysian American? Miraculously, not at all. Redding, a lapsed guitarist, is gloriously, shudderingly straightforward on bass: no flash, no fucking about. His fuzzy elemental rumble will be at the heart of this (new term) *power trio*. Mitchell, meanwhile, like Led Zeppelin's John Bonham and Black Sabbath's Bill Ward, is coming out of R&B and jazz—he idolizes Elvin Jones particularly—but with futuristic weight, with the swing that will become real heaviness. (No heaviness without swing.) Perhaps he's the only drummer in England capable of tracking his new singer/guitarist into the Hendrixian sound-world.

And that sound-world, as it touches down in Swinging London, is already full-formed. Blues ghosts electrically summoned; interstellar turbulence; fringed-with-incineration flights and passages of liquid gentleness; a technique that combines towering phallic exhibition with an uncanny, almost ego-less surrender to the possibilities of his instrument.

The possibilities. Oh, the possibilities. Technology is one of his muses, pulling him forward: amplification, overdrive, the loudest stack, the latest gear, the only-just-invented. Roger Mayer, who will design and customize effects pedals for him, is an acoustic engineer for the British Navy. If you want to sound like Jimi Hendrix, Frank Zappa explains to the readers of *LIFE* magazine in 1968, "buy a Fender Stratocaster, an Arbiter Fuzz Face, a Vox Wah-Wah Pedal, and four Marshall amplifiers."

So much for the hardware: the thing, the event, the breakthrough, is what he *does* with it. Having stroked and pelvically jostled his guitar to a state of glimmering, agonized sensitivity, Hendrix sculpts the resulting feedback with his shoulders and extralarge hands. Feedback: the gremlin of amplification, which has tormented guitarists since they first plugged in. Hendrix befriends it—romances it. He conducts it, in both senses of the word: it is carried by his body. He has a supple and godlike relationship with ELECTRICITY.

His solos can be astral dramas or inside jokes. At his feet the pale cohort of London guitar heroes—Beck, Page, Townshend—turns paler still. Eric Clapton's hand, as he lights his cigarette after a guitar duel with Hendrix, is shaking. The Rolling Stones's Brian Jones, at every Jimi Hendrix Experience show he attends, will punctually weep for joy. A beautiful image from Norman's *Wild Thing*: "In whatever dark London vault the Experience played, [Jones] would be visible as a dual glint of blond hair and tear-wet cheeks."

Hendrix writes whooshing, crazily orchestrated hippie rock. He's bonkers about Dylan. But what he is, fundamentally, is a bluesman. The blues are his school and his laboratory, the spine of his wildness. And he doesn't just play the blues, Jimi Hendrix *has* the blues: on at least a portion of his prismatic personality the blues are clanging down all day, a hail of Bibles and grand pianos. Because he's a bluesman, his pain is a historical burden. But his pain is also private, motherless Seattle winters that turned the infant Hendrix blue with cold. It's one of the more lethal ironies of his art: here's a human truly alive, a paragon of feeling, who continually confesses his numbness, his down-ness, his separation from himself. Who writes a song called "I Don't Live Today."

So confusion swirls around him, sends him up and down, purple-hazes him, and it'll get him in the end. Pretty soon, in fact. But not before he's recorded the greatest rock song, the most electrified guitar performance, of all: "Voodoo Chile (Slight Return)."

Writing, words, should pause here. To write about his sound, the actual *noise-in-your-body* of Jimi Hendrix? Well now. There's a theme to beggar your lexicon and freeze you at the frontiers of sense. Still, what's writing for, if not to fling itself at the unwritable?

"Voodoo Chile (Slight Return)" is the final track on *Electric Ladyland*. The song's intro, those snickering accents flicked from deadened strings, is almost pre-musical—it sounds like something scratching at the inside of an eggshell. The melody is announced, in notes opulent with wah-wah; Mitch Mitchell flexes his hi-hat; then, with a rattlesnake shake of maracas, Hendrix takes a leering plunge into distortion—tuned down, E7 sharp 9, the "Hendrix chord." After three bars the guitar rears up again, pluming monstrously with energy; after four Hendrix time-travels, flipping his toggle switch back and forth to create a sound like passing space-freight . . . And here comes the voice, supernaturally authorized, hugely doubled by his guitar.

This Hendrix, this singer, is an immense and magical figure. A smasher of mountains. By the end of the song the mix is panning wildly, desperately, as if overwhelmed by its own information, sizzling up into near deafness before widening downward in a welter of noise.

The mountain-fragments, the mind-fragments have formed a new shape.

Now we're electric. Forever.

ODE TO THE PERSISTENCE OF EVIL IN THE HUMAN HEART

That the Devil is within me

I have evidence enough:

when I see men on ladders

I want them to fall off.

ODE TO CRYING WHILE FLYING

They say it's the thinness of the oxygen, don't they, or the altitude, or some depressurizing in the brain or something. It makes us more weepy.

But the tears that you shed at 30,000 feet are real. Realer perhaps, richer and heavier, than the tears you shed on the ground. Crying while flying: it's deep.

Not to discount the environment. The environment is crucial. The environment, that is, of being strapped in, with strangers, enveloped in ambient plane-whoosh, sailing over a carpet of air pockets like bubble wrap. Above the seat in front of you the crown of somebody's head is wobbling with tiny travel shocks. Flight attendants, the guardians of this environment, beacons of sanity and formality, pass splendidly up and down the aisle.

Meanwhile, outside your window/porthole/peep-hole . . . Wild light. Celestial upholstery. The intimate parts of clouds. Zooming birth-pang brightness and soft unearthly tones. Up here you're in Swedenborg-land. Emanuel Swedenborg, that is: the eighteenth-century Swedish mystic who was regularly plucked into heaven to converse with the angels. The angels, he said, would impart to him "things . . . inexpressible except simply by shiftings of a heavenly light—not at all by human words." His number one fan was William Blake.

So you're in a mad place. And one of the attributes of this place, you discover, is that while you're in it you can watch a not-so-great movie, even kind of a shitty movie, and be—reduced to tears? No. Increased to tears. Amplified and expanded to tears. You can appreciate this movie with a full heart and wetly shining cheeks. You can watch *Independence Day* and well up dramatically. Or you can watch a good, solid, right-down-the-middle movie, an old friend—*Mrs. Doubtfire*, *Good Will Hunting*—and bring scaldingly fresh dollops of emotion to it. "Will . . . Listen to me, son. It's *not your fault*." Let it flow!

What's going on? Well, you've been released. Released from your corny terrestrial prejudices. Released into your own wonderful coarseness and sentimentality. Released, with mellowed faculties and uncorked geysers of feeling, to as-if-drunkenly (or just drunkenly) embrace the art that is being offered to you. You're watching movies like the angels do.

As of this writing, the last movie I cried at on a plane was *Dog*, starring Channing Tatum. On the ground, this movie is a semi-turkey, or at least it has turkey aspects. It's basically flightless. But in the air, oh my God. It spreads its beautiful wings. The themes of grief and injury and fellowship. The innocent handsomeness of Channing Tatum, and his balletic parkour-y stuntman grace as he skis on his heels down a wooded slope in pursuit of his runaway dog . . . I was a wreck. I was smothered in tears, gasping, as if a couple of extra valves had opened in my face.

Of course you don't have to be watching a movie to cry while flying. Plenty of other stuff to cry about. On one long-ago flight I burst into tears, with biological promptness, every twenty minutes. Life issues. Brain issues. Again, it was the flight itself, the fact of being in the air, that licensed these breakouts.

And let's give thanks, while we're at it, for the flight attendants. For the big brassy hellos as we all file onto the plane, and the smaller, lines-around-the-eyes goodbyes as we all file off again, having got to know one other a little better. For the canned speeches over the inflight PA—always somehow invested with a fillip of real feeling—and the limp theater of the safety demonstration, the long-suffering puff into the tiny tube on the lifejacket. For the courtesy, even when (especially when) it is feigned or forced. For the entire ceremony of flying, the ritual space—created and maintained by the flight attendants—in which you can have your big cry.

Think about what they do up there. They minister, they mollify, they bring blankets, they deal with alcoholics and exploding parents and rude fuckers and then they walk around with a plastic bag, collecting trash. Have I been a good passenger, over the years? Not too needy? Thankful where appropriate? I hope so. There was that crying-every-twenty-minutes flight. And the flight where I wore a jacket that stank so vengefully of cat piss that the man next to me asked to change seats.

So bless the flight attendants, cat-piss-free, keeping it together so you can fall to pieces. Bless the altitude, bless the seat, bless the golden loft-space above the clouds, bless the screen six inches from your nose. Bless the little bottle of red wine. Bless Emanuel Swedenborg, peeping in your window. Bless Channing Tatum. And, most forgivingly, rain blessings upon your own way-up-there destroyed-by-weeping self.

ODE TO SITTING THERE

You've never heard of him.

In the folk memory of New England psychiatry, he looms spherical and silvery-paternal, puffing a kindly pipe. A healer, a teacher, a one-man band of clinical humanism: Dr. Elvin Semrad. At his approach, it is told, the beside-themselves would find themselves, and the nonsense-talkers magically begin to make sense. A generation of trainee psychiatrists sat in awe.

But he's not in *your* canon, non-shrink reader, because he wrote no books, cured no celebrities, gave his name to no large theory. His aphorisms, his in-passing Semradisms, were noted down on the fly by students anxious that they not be forgotten. Example: "I don't know of any human beings that are free—they all have to make up their minds if they're going to stay with Judy or go to work."

Semrad was clinical director of the Massachusetts Mental Health Center, a.k.a. Mass Mental, from 1956 until shortly before his death in 1976. "Mass

Mental was a public institution," says Stephen Berg-man, who trained under Semrad in the early '70s and later—as Samuel Shem—wrote the best-selling novel *House of God*. "So it got all kinds of patients and some very serious mental illness. Psychotics, schizophrenics, manic depressives, suicidal people. It was a rough place, not squeaky clean at all." And every year twenty-five psychiatric residents would enter, blinking, to learn their trade.

Semrad supervised, he guided and encouraged, he set the tone. Now and again he lectured. The Semrad of memory is white-mustached and bel-lied like the Buddha, shedding rays of teacherly benignity from an almost-always-open office door. "Everybody loved him," Bergman says. "A rumpled, roly-poly Father Christmas. It was like talking to your grandfather—who is finally listen-ing to you, for a change."

But it was around his famous case conferences that the myth of Semrad clustered and grew. To the twenty-first-century layman, the case conference sounds a little iffy: A lone patient would be "pre-sented" to a roomful of students and professionals by his or her therapist and then interviewed, in front of everybody, by Semrad—after which, still in front of everybody, Semrad would discuss the case with the therapist. High psychiatric theater, you might say, with some fairly obvious structural negatives for the patient.

Nonetheless, the case conference was a standard feature of psychiatric training at the time, and occasionally a useful teaching tool. Besides, in the aura of Dr. Semrad, its artificialities seemed to be dissolved, or at least suspended. Here he would showcase his celebrated rapport with the unreachable. Over a patient who might be jittery with psychosis, or schizophrenically abstract, Semrad would calmly open the battered old umbrella of the everyday. "He could sit down with a patient with 25 people watching him," remembers Aaron Lazare, who trained at Mass Mental and went on to be chancellor and dean of UMass Medical School in Worcester, "and it was like two men sitting on a park bench, just talking. He would get to the heart of the matter. And I was really stunned by that. I said, 'This is gonna be my teacher.'"

Onstage, Semrad would take the patient on his patented "tour of the body," asking them where, physically, they could locate the sensation that was bothering them: in the head, in the stomach, in the chest? If the latter, Semrad might suggest—courteously—that the patient was suffering from a broken heart. (Jerry Gans, a former Semrad pupil who today practices in Wellesley, once tried this on a particularly intractable Mass Mental patient. Her response: "Don't give me any of that Semrad shit!") The body—its reactions, its rebellions—was central in his system, because the body doesn't lie. "This is what makes the difference, the *tissues* of the persons involved," he said, "not the fancy thoughts upstairs."

There was a formidable technical-clinical apparatus undergirding Semrad's approach, decades of experience and training at work. Gerald Adler, in his paper "The Psychotherapy of Schizophrenia: Semrad's Contributions to Current Psychoanalytic Concepts," refers to Semrad's "vast array of techniques that responded to the patient's fear, through the support of the patient's autonomy. . . . He constantly reminded the patient that the patient had an observing ego, though rudimentary, and expected the patient to assume optimal responsibility for his feelings, wishes, and predicament." As a teacher Semrad was not above shoptalk ("A functioning ego split is necessary to interrupt character syntonicity"), and he wrote or cowrote a number of academic papers that are, it is generally agreed, unreadable.

In person, however, and above all with patients, he was atheoretical. With patients he used no jargon—or if he did, it was the jargon of the everyday: the marketplace "(Are you willing to pay the price for what you want?") and sometimes the farmyard ("If the shit is collecting in the barn, you've got to shovel it out. Otherwise before you know it the barn will be full and you won't be able to manage it").

And there was a kind of exotic gallantry, at the case conferences, in his treatment of patients. "In that room," says Jerry Gans, "there are seven of us highly trained residents, nurses, social workers, occupational therapists, and then there's the broken-down patient. And Semrad would say to the patient, 'Do I have your permission to talk with these young people about how we might think about what you've told us today, and how we might help you?' And the *respect* embedded in that question had a profound effect on me. A lot of his teaching was indirect like that." The courtesy, the formality, was an offering to the autonomy of the patient. "How did you arrange it for yourself to be brought here?" he might ask the newly arrived—and perhaps utterly disoriented—Mass Mental inmate.

In the confrontation or casting out of demons, a certain bounceresque affability and restraint will come in handy. Jesus, for example, was pretty good at it. His castings-out, his psychospiritual heave-hos, were accomplished not with towering exorcisms and special effects but with a firm quiet word, the biblical equivalent of "All right, sunshine, out you go."

There is something of this in any good shrink, and there was an extraordinary amount of it in Semrad. "There's no reason to think that in spending half an hour with a patient there's going to be any radical and permanent change," Gans says. "It was more watching him with the person. In order to relate to some of these patients, you had to get in touch with parts of yourself that you'd had the luxury of not getting in touch with before, and it could be pretty rough. There was something about his way of being that was hard to explicate, but you knew that something powerful was happening."

No tricks. No quaking curative breakthroughs. The confusion or fragmentation of the patient would be met with a sort of dogmatic wholeness. "Don't you believe what you feel?" Semrad would ask. "It's pretty bad if a man can't believe in himself." Or, he would challenge, "Can you prove it? If you can prove it, I'll believe it."

Here we touch upon a paradox of Semrad—the ineffable solidity, the unwobbling personal substance that took on, in the moment of encounter, a transcendent value. "He wasn't mystical at all," says Susan Rako, the Newtonville psychiatrist and author who with fellow Semrad pupil Harvey Mazer compiled *Semrad: The Heart of a Therapist*, a collection of his sayings. "He was very grounded, very real. He had fat ankles. He wore white socks and black shoes."

The typical Semradism rides the wild edge between Zen mind-zap and rustic commonplace: You could tack up one or two of them right next to *You don't have to be crazy to work here—but it helps!* "Occasionally," writes Mazer in the introduction to *Semrad: Heart of a Therapist*, "I would wonder whether he

had lifted them directly from the *Reader's Digest*."
But at its most proverbial, the Semradism is simply
common sense, cubed. "If you have to tell someone something, it's already too late." Chew on that
for a while.

By his disposition and presence Semrad signaled—at
the deepest level—that he wasn't going anywhere.
To his pupils he would talk of "putting a floor
under a patient." And the patients, as if miraculously, would calm down, or open up. Therapists
at the demonstration interviews would routinely
hear their patients tell Semrad things, after ten
minutes, that they themselves had been unable to
elicit in months of treatment. "That was one of
the most powerful teaching points for me," Gans
says. "It left me with the question, 'Is there something about me and the way I was approaching the
patient that is keeping this material from emerg-
ing?' And I think that's a really important question
for a therapist."

"Elvin Semrad, in spite of the influence he had in
his own time, has been gradually forgotten," wrote
Joel Paris in his 2005 book *The Fall of an Icon: Psychoanalysis and Academic Psychiatry*. "One reason is
that he worked in oral culture, and wrote almost
nothing. The other is that his ideas were never
supported by data. Semrad was a guru, but most
young psychiatrists today would not even recognize
his name."

Is this the Semrad of history—trapped there, dwindling into psychiatry's yesteryear? For sure, there's been an ideological sea change since his day. Psychiatry is no longer dominated, as it was in Semrad's time, by psychoanalysis. And even during Semrad's lifetime, the ground was beginning to shift beneath his feet. For him, as for many of his peers, the burgeoning fields of neurobiology and psychopharmacology held little interest, and most medication was "poison."

"He seemed to help people," Stephen Bergman says. "And that's the good news. Because it's good to help people in a 40-minute interview. And he was very modest; he didn't stand up and take a bow. The bad news, frankly, is that the generation of psychiatrists that he taught took away from that that there was a psychoanalytic-based treatment for severe psychosis, schizophrenia, manic depression, and severe depression."

The data don't support Semrad. So far. Chemistry is required. Or is it? This could be a scientific question, or a moral one, or both. We live in an age between ages. Are there places in the mind, in the heart, where the angels of sanity cannot go? Semrad thought not. As Susan Rako says, "You can *always* relate."

What, then, is the legacy, the Semradic transmission? "You've got to love your patients," he said, the point being that otherwise you won't have the faintest hope of understanding them. Which isn't just good therapy: it's a law of human relations. Narrow your eyes at somebody, narrow the categories into which you're fitting them, and you're getting a tenth of the information you need. But receive them openly, really openly, eyes wide and heart wide, and you'll get it all: what's noble about them, what's dangerous about them, where they might be trying to deceive you, or deceiving themselves.

Leston Havens, in a 1983 lecture, said that Semrad—in privileging the patient's feelings, and in his resistance to interpretation, extrapolation, psychological glibness—"turned the procedures of psychotherapy upside down." The elevation of Semrad into a larger-than-life figure, in Havens's telling, was a trick the world played on him: "The world made him a guru, a venerable one . . . so that the world would not have to confront what he meant. They would only have to confront *him*. His message disappeared into his person. And it was safe in his person."

And the person is gone, leaving this rather basic but somehow mysterious heat imprint on the history of psychiatry. It may fade, even as his acolytes quote him, channel him, remember him. But when he was present—in his supreme patience, in his undemonstrative commerce with the way, way out—he was really, truly, radically present. So perhaps to be Semradian means simply this: to sit there.

And stay there.

ODE TO WANTING TO
BE A GREAT POET

O let me write a deathless lyric,
like A. E. Housman or Robert Herrick.
Just one. Just for fun.
And then I'm done.

ODE TO DESPAIR AS A VERB

You don't want to do it too often. To allow failure, that is, to break over you in a freezing black wave. To confess in your inmost inmostness that the project of *you*, so hopefully conceived, has never really succeeded, is certainly not succeeding now, and has—let's face it—no very realistic prospect of succeeding in the future.

One must limit one's exposure to this kind of thing. It puts a strain on the immune system.

But now and again you have to go there. You have to taste the tastelessness. You have to abandon yourself to abandonment. You have to despair.

Despair is a noun. It's a condition and it's a place. It's the graveyard in Matthew's Gospel where the Gerasene demoniac, the man possessed by an evil spirit, sits and chafes in his chains and bangs his rocks tonelessly together—*tonk, tonk, tonk*—and waits, without knowing it, for Jesus. In despair you join this exiled immobilized man and you sit next to him, in your own chains, among the tombs of your own forebears, banging your own rocks together. *Tonk, tonk, tonk.*

But despair is also a verb. You *do* it: dispense with consolation, dispense with self-preservation, dump it all and despair. And here's the point: If you can despair, you can un-despair. Or rather you can *be* un-despaired. Because in despairing, in collapsing as an act of will, there is a surrender. And after surrender: possibility.

I can testify to this. By opening yourself to the cold nasty current of disintegration and discouragement that runs six inches beneath the surface of existence, you make yourself available to that other, deeper current: the one that warms and heartens and shapes and sustains. It's right there. It knows who you are. And on the far side of despair, it will reach for you.

ODE TO FRIDGE HUM

It lies at the bottom of all things, when the talking's stopped, and the household fidgetings and flappings are over, and the gyre of world din is stilled. Four a.m.: Hold your apartment to your ear like a seashell, and what do you hear? Fridge hum.

Non-human. Steady. Although not without nuance: sometimes it contains a climbing, whining, reaching frequency. And the brain, once tuned in, will insist on finding a pattern, on trying to make music out of it: minimalist vibes, Terry Riley chimes, or some kind of electrically attenuated raga. You feel there's an invitation in there somewhere, if only to sit on the kitchen floor and drone along in sympathy. And of course it clicks on and off. On, and it's as if it's always been there. Off, and it leaves a suction of quiet behind it.

I'm not one of nature's Buddhists. I'm too attached to the polluted incorrigible Western self, the self that masturbates and writes novels. Emptiness worries me. But I appreciate the beauty of it, and the necessity. And one afternoon I found myself in a chanting circle led by a Buddhist nun. *Om mani padme hum* was the chant, the mantra, and round and round me it went, looping and deepening in grandeur and significance even as I tried and failed to open my knotted little larynx to it. Repetition is holy. I strained. I felt discomfort. Oh, narrow aperture of man. Oh, constricted throat, constricted vessel. Oh egocentricity. Let the chant be chanted. Let it chant itself!

Om mani padme hum . . . *Om mani padme hum* . . . We were summoning the jewel in the lotos or (to my understanding) the power-drone of love at the bottom of the universe. But is it love or is it fridge hum? What if fridge hum, cold alien fridge hum, is the noise between the stars? The stars, the stars. I happen to believe that they're diagrammed in love, those jabs and flutters of light.

But what do I know?

ODE TO PROCRASTINATION

Mysterious state, more passive than active.

When you're procrastinating, stalling, temporizing, fucking about, it envelops you. You are consumed by the thing you're not doing. The commitment you're resisting. It niggles in your brain, it itches in your body. As for your soul: some kind of invisible celestial countdown is going on somewhere. Tick, tick, tick.

And there's something schizoid about it, too.

Outwardly, when I'm procrastinating, I'm at my ease: I'm pottering about, I'm picking up books and putting them down again, I'm chatting gaily on the phone, I'm eating BBQ chips. But inwardly, inwardly, I'm in violent Luciferian rebellion against the angels of adulthood, of responsibility, of unfreedom. I'm clenched, I'm sulphurous. I brood, with fiery pinions. I *won't* go to the bloody bank. I won't go to the post office. I might not shave. Expecting something from me? Feedback? A prompt reply? A timely handling of something-or-other? Good luck.

That's Phase One: clinically interesting, but no fun. Sloth, like every sin worth the name, disquiets me and divides me from myself. And the early stage of procrastination is suffused with sloth.

The horizon brightens, however, in Phase Two. In Phase Two you get busy. Vats of energy are suddenly available to you. Straining to avoid that one particular thing, dawdling mightily, you can do five other things. You can clean the house. You can work out. You can write a book. The wrong book, but still—a book. If you organize yourself skillfully, you can be productive and even sort of professional *precisely while not doing what you're supposed to be doing.* My friend Josh calls this "the virtuous circle of procrastination."

In Phase Three it ends. It has to. Strangely built in to the procrastinatory moment, however long it lasts, is the consciousness that eventually, finally, you are going to do this thing. You may have dallied with magical thinking (perhaps they'll forget about it . . . perhaps somebody *else* will do it) but you know there's no way out. It's going to happen. So bring on the Red Bull, bring on the Slayer, the deadline, the freakout and the perspiration, whatever it takes. Sometimes all it takes is literally forty-five seconds of sustained attention. How about *that*?

And now it's over. You've emerged. You've been playing with Time like a weird little god, stretching it and inspecting it. And you'll do it again, procrastinator, you know you will, until there's no more time to play with.

ODE TO NOT DRINKING

I note the change when I resist
my alcoholic whim.
The mornings are more sparkling
but the evenings are more dim.

ODE TO HUGS

Not everyone likes them as much as I do.

I know that. Why should they? And I'm not totally crass: I am aware, sometimes, as I blunder in open-armed, as I surge uninvited into the ozone of another's bosom, of being received with a certain diffidence or stillness. There are non-huggers in the world. They exist.

But me, I'm wired for hugs and there's not a lot I can do about it. Full contact, lingering pressure, the works. With sound effects, if possible—a communion of groans, ribcage to rumbling ribcage. That's the kind of hug I'm always looking for.

It was Ecstasy that set me off, or opened me up, back in the raving '90s. In the clubs, in the warehouses, in the cellars of houses in the East End of London, I was a drug hugger. A hugging bug. Frug, drug, bug and then get snug in a hug. Shambling in bliss across those laser-tormented dance floors, floating through twists of dry ice with my eyes turned to dizzy black discs, absolved from Englishness, absolved from private education, magically licensed to throw my arms around the nearest hard-looking rave geezer . . . What a feeling.

And the feeling was reciprocated, that was the point. Equally deranged by pills, equally fraternally off-his-tits, the hard-looking rave geezer would hug me back. On a beach in California, beats pinging and bass belching in the air around us, a dreadlocked stranger placed his hands upon my shoulders, gazed deep, deep, *deep* into my eyes and said (Northern Irish accent): "I don't know who y'are . . . But I focking LOVE YA." Then we hugged, and he entered my brain chemistry. Entered it and altered it.

Long ago, long ago. But the hugs remain. As does the altered chemistry. My son was telling me the other day, in a guess-what way, about the efficiency with which cocaine blocks the brain's serotonin transporters. ("It's kind of genius, dad.") I panicked: "Serotonin?! Jesus Christ, son, don't mess with your serotonin! Listen to me. That stuff is like God's maple syrup in your brain. He gives you a lifetime supply, but only if you don't fuck about with it."

Not especially scientific, I know, but that's how I feel about the hormone serotonin, the good-vibes regulator. It's an actual chemical that exists, measurably, in the brain. But it's also a metaphor. Half-substance, half-spirit. Like us.

And indeed I did fuck about with my ration of serotonin, my God-given happiness allowance. Gobbling Ecstasy and gorging myself on cheapo dance-floor love, I went into serotonin debt. I squandered and sizzled up half a lifetime's worth of gentle contentments in a few euphoric spikes, a few combustions of the ego, a few mad and melting hugs. And I felt it, the deficit, like a leaky or fire-blackened room at the back of my brain, for the next ten years.

When I think about the non-huggers, the not-to-be-hugged, I think of the wavelet of genius Germans who washed up in Los Angeles in the '30s, in flight from the Nazis: slovenly Brecht, severe Adorno, all-spikes Schoenberg, master of dissonance. To a man they deplored the local strain of bonhomie: The backslapping, the heavy fellowship. The goddamn Californian positivity. "It is difficult for us to smile incessantly," complained Schoenberg. My hug-habits would have appalled him.

And I get it, the anti-hug argument. Barging in for a hug . . . There's an oppression to it, an indelicacy, an unreflecting maleness even. But here's the thing: I love all that. In fact I think it saved my ass. In the hugged-up maelstrom of American heavy fellowship, I—Englishman with a starved brain—have been redeemed.

Good bouncers know about hugging. At a metal show in Cambridge, Massachusetts, I saw a huge bouncer wade gently into the pit and wrap his arms around an especially violent and selfish dancer. This kid had been all over the place, limbs everywhere, a private veering tornado-cone. But now, in the embrace of the bouncer, he was quieted. It was as if this is what he wanted. As if it was *all* he wanted—to be held, enveloped, embosomed. Re-enfolded in imperturbable brotherhood. He went limp, and was harmlessly released.

And people like me, when you hug us, when we've come at you with our neurotic overspill of affection and contact-need, and you hold us tight, a similar thing happens: We are settled. We are contained and made calm.

"The world is not comprehensible," said Martin Buber, "but it is embraceable." Ditto: humans.

ODE TO THE RAVERS

Out of the furnace of embraces
we come with wizened pre-dawn faces.
We've been transfigured many a time
by many a pill and many a chime,
travelling to parts of London that are odd
to ring ourselves like angels
around a white-hot invisible
chemical embryo-god.

We see by laser, we see by strobe,
we search out your soul with synthetic probe.
All night, all night, all night, all night,
with eyes unnaturally bright,
twisting the ancient oscillator
we track that shifting bleep
and never sleep.
Sometimes we're lairy,
sometimes arms-in-the-airy:
prisoners of bliss are we.
In the cave of smoke, with our fairy folk,
some flash of the last drug-energy
races across our blackening grid
and daylight lowers its lid.

ODE TO LUCK

Chance, felicity, providence, weal . . . It does give us some variations, my buxom and ever-generous thesaurus. But I still think there should be more words for *luck*.

Or perhaps the same amount of words, but with more precise definitions. The Germans, I'm told, have a single enormous word for the experience of stepping off the curb and being narrowly missed by a speeding bicycle. And another one for the sensation of finding a seat in a packed subway car and realizing, at the same moment, that the person sitting next to you is vibrantly insane. We need words like these in English.

Because luck is a great mystery. *The* great mystery, in a way. It makes things happen, or not happen, to deserving or undeserving people. I mean: is it real at all, luck? Or is it just a word for things not making sense?

It's about physics: the tumbling ball that gives you the winning lottery number (good luck) and the air conditioner that falls on your head (bad luck) are both subject to the same set of laws.

But it's also about the psyche. *You make your own luck.* Nonsense, right? And yet we know it to be true. For example: cartoon luck, Buster Keaton luck, miraculous angelic-idiotic stepping-from-the-wreckage-without-a-scratch luck. People are often granted this kind of luck as a reward for courage and/or good humour. Or Freudian luck, which is where your neurosis, malign wizard, conjures actual purpose-built real-world incidents and accidents to daunt and tickle and bother you.

And then—most cosmic, most fateful—there's Blakeian luck: "Some are born to sweet delight/ Some are born to endless night." Got good genes, nice parents? Lucky, lucky you. The opposite, endless night, is what Lou Reed was singing about in his great junkie elegy "Street Hassle": a condition of spiritual disadvantage, of being crocked from the beginning, from before the beginning, trapped in the terrible choices of people who never had a choice. You know what it's called, he asks? Bad luck.

Great soccer players, at their great moments, generate fields of luck around themselves: specialized fluky football luck. The ball dings off somebody's shin and goes just the right way ("It bounced kindly for him," as the announcers say); the stutter or stumble becomes a flutter of pure skill. It has to do with nerve, it has to do with balance, it has to do with appetite. A goal-snatcher like Luis Suarez seemed in his prime especially favoured by this kind of slippery almost sleazy good fortune. He pressed, squirmed, nibbled, darted, grabbed, wrangled, molested, cheated; he fed on opportunity.

And lo, she smiled upon him: promiscuous and rapacious Lady Luck. He was her true son. Events and micro-events bent towards him. Always in the thick of it, always battling, Suarez was (almost) never injured. He was capable of beautiful football: long, smoking strikes; crazy-making solo runs; crackling telepathy with his teammates, inside a hive of tight passes. But the essential Suarez goal was short-range, larcenous, and inflected with chaos—which is one of the faces of luck.

January 12, 2014. Liverpool are in the thirty-first minute of a fixture against lower-table battlers Stoke. They have already scored once, from a nasty deflection—luck is with them. And now the scowling Martin Skrtel, top goon of Liverpool's back line, sends the ball up and across the pitch, left to right. The speculative drive, the long ball—the least subtle and most condescended-to ball in soccer, generally described as having been "hoofed," "clattered," "thumped" or (less often) "blootered" upfield.

But as Skrtel's ball floats into the Stoke eighteen-yard box, heat-seeking Suarez has already locked on. It takes a huge bounce; Suarez bears down; Stoke defender Marc Wilson rises like a startled pheasant and tries to head it back to his goalkeeper, Jack Butland. The header is too weak; the ball drifts; Suarez scuttles past Wilson, his eyes raised and goal-drool already shining on his chin. Stoke enforcer Ryan Shawcross lumbers across, droning with imminent damage, but his attempt to sweep the ball away from the Suarez of the present turns out to be a neat pass to the Suarez who lives two seconds into the future—who jinks, gathers, fends off a half-hearted embrace from Shawcross, and with his first touch slides the ball under Butland's outflung left leg.

The back of the net receives it with a sigh. Butland tastes grass and ashes, Shawcross looks blackly at Wilson, Wilson's face is a potato of disbelief. And Suarez arcs away, rejoicing. Is it beauty? No, it is not beauty. It is greed, hazard, readiness, delight in error. It's luck.

Or let's look at another great Liverpool player, another striker: Mo Salah.

Salah, as a personality on the pitch, a personality in the game, is un-Suarez. Ego is not detectable. Desire itself seems to be a low vibration—mere wistfulness, as it might appear. When not involved in the play he can seem to be drifting, just bobbing about non-assertively under his Mo Salah hairstyle, his twin bulbs of side-frizz.

But then: October 3, 2021, Liverpool against Manchester City. Seventy-sixth minute. There's Salah, just outside the City penalty area, thoughtful, floating in his zone of mild potential. Dangerous-looking? Not at all. But oh, how luck-available he is. How ready for its wild currents.

He takes a short pass from Curtis Jones. Immediately he is pressed, spikily impinged upon by City's Joao Cancelo. He repels the challenge, bounces Cancelo away and spins around, ball at his feet, into no space at all: blue shirts everywhere, the City defence contracting upon him like a lens. Now with preposterous suavity he passes his left foot over the ball and rolls it onto his right, producing an illusionist's teeny-weeny lesion in spacetime, a trick which has the effect of making City's Bernardo Silva—sublimely intelligent and combative footballer Bernardo Silva—sit down, as if in surprise. Salah, with three defenders still between him and the goal, is now possessed: by luck, by art, by the magnetism of what must be. He is untouchable.

The City players meanwhile are finding themselves in a hostile matrix, in feedback. Ruben Dias, Aymeric Laporte: they clank, they grind, they groan, they fall over. They're deafened. Bad luck everywhere. He's gone through them all now, and with his right foot left-footed Salah drives the ball across the City goal, across the gaping goalkeeper Ederson, and into the far corner. Time ripples backward, reclaiming the previous ten seconds and sealing them in perfection. Goal.

One word for Salah luck. Another word for Suarez luck. Still other words for your luck and my luck and "Street Hassle" luck. Here's how I see it: luck is the static rubbed up by the mere friction of human existence, by all of us acting and not acting on each other, loving and squabbling and giving parking tickets, and it hovers about in prickly clouds, looking for conductors. Then it strikes. Into the atomic muddle of life, or of a soccer match, it sends a spark and creates a pattern. Instantly.

Can you work with it, befriend it, get it on your side? Hear the *crump* of the air conditioner as it lands on the sidewalk three inches behind you? Sail out of the birth canal into a realm of sweet delight? Dump Bernardo Silva on his ass and score a legendary goal?

Sure you can. If you're lucky.

ODE TO THE LOST CUP OF TEA

There are degrees of lostness. Dimensions of lostness. Our small black cat, Tony, when we can't
find him, will seem to have winked out of existence entirely—to have removed himself from
time and space, leaving not even the twang of
absence behind him. Not only will he not be
found: he was never here.

The half-drunk cup of tea is not like this. It's
somewhere—definitely, discomfitingly—but where?
You put it down thirty seconds ago, on one of your
aimless automaton rambles around your apartment,
and now you can't find it. Shelf, sill, countertop?
Edge of the bathroom sink? You feel its proximity,
its pressure, the shallowness of its concealment and
its yearning to be discovered. You're also conscious,
as you diddle about from room to room, of the
thermodynamics of the situation: the small catas-
trophe of its cooling-down. Cold tea. Not good.

Is it worth bothering Anthony of Padua, patron
saint of lost objects, with this? Does he need to get
involved? Maybe he does, because you're growing
frantic. Your universe is unravelling. Somewhere

there's a space-hole full of black cats and single socks and rogue sets of car keys. Up goes the prayer:

> *Saint Anthony, Saint Anthony,*
> *you see me searching anxiously,*
> *you know that without your intercession*
> *I'll sink into chaos and low-grade depression.*
>
> *So find it for me, Saint Anthony.*
> *Part the clouds of obscurity.*
> *And if my* [insert missing item] *you*
>   *can't restore,*
> *then let me not worry about it anymore.*

What does he actually *do*, Saint Anthony? Does he work with the lost object itself, heightening the contrast around it and making it glowingly visible to your bleary eye? Or does he work inside your brain, making you remember, throwing back beams of awareness into the dopey state in which you mislaid whatever it is you're looking for?

Well, however he does it, he gets it done. A couple more shambling, swearing, prayerful laps of the apartment and—there it is. Your cup of tea. Sitting pertly and with exaggerated innocence on a pile of magazines. Two tepid swallows, and everything's OK again.

Crisis over. You're whole.

ODE TO THE LONELINESS
OF THE MOON

The moon came down to the pub one night
and everyone wanted to fight him.
One look at that face, so pitted and white,
and the mildest man hankered to smite him.

He stood at the bar with a pint in his hand,
swivelling his moony stare,
and the ray of his rampant anonymous eye
provoked every drinker in there.

Poor pallid old moon, poor pitiful moon,
the bartender asked him to leave.
So he floated, rejected, back into the sky,
there to shine, and to shine, and to grieve.

ODE TO DIFFICULT PEOPLE

One way to understand the saints, those glorious freaks, is to imagine them as cutting-edge physicists.

Ordinary, B-plus, taken-for-granted reality, the place where most of us live . . . They go right through it. Right through the veil of muddle and into the essential structures. Or non-structures, because the world as they see it is hollowed out and illumined by beams of divine love. And also upside-down. The first shall be last and the last shall be first. He who wishes to save his life will lose it. Blessed are the poor in spirit. And to flash out with the first blast of the creating Word—should you wish to do so—is merely to live in accordance with these principles.

Whether or not the Catholic Church makes it official—and the cause for her canonization rumbles on—Dorothy Day was most definitely a saint. *Is* a saint, because the saints keep going, keep provoking, keep being difficult: that's what they're for. Day, who died aged eighty-three in in 1980, was about people, especially poor people, especially

what she called with some wryness "the undeserving poor," and the paramount importance of
serving them. For her what the Church defines as
the Works of Mercy—feed the hungry, clothe the
naked, shelter the homeless, and so on—were not
pious injunctions or ways to be nice. They were
atomic decrees.

How did she arrive at such a place? Let's go to
the montage.

Here's Greenwich Village Dorothy, apprentice
journalist, in 1916: She is "cool-mannered," as her
granddaughter Kate Hennessy writes in *The World
Will Be Saved by Beauty*, "tweed-wearing, drinking rye whiskey with no discernible effect." She's
with her buddy Eugene O'Neill—*the* Eugene
O'Neill—in a bar called the Hell Hole. O'Neill,
with "bitter mouth" and "monotonous grating
voice" is reciting one of his favorite poems: Francis
Thompson's "The Hound of Heaven." *I fled Him,
down the nights and down the days; / I fled Him down
the arches of the years.* Chased by God. By way of
response, Dorothy sings a Jimmie Rodgers song:
Frankie and Johnny were sweethearts . . .

Here's Dorothy a year later, lying in darkness on a
work-farm bunk in Virginia, on hunger strike, having been arrested, beaten, and terrorized for joining
a picket line of suffragists. ("I lost all consciousness
of any cause," she would write of this episode in

her memoir *The Long Loneliness*. "I had no sense of being a radical, making protest. . . . The futility of life came over me so that I could not weep but only lie there in blank misery.")

Here she is in 1922 in Chicago, "fling[ing] herself about" in the wake of an abortion, a failed marriage, and a suicide attempt. She's in love, at this point, with a pugilistic, alpha-male newspaperman called Lionel Moise. And here she is in the winter of 1933, on the Lower East Side, with Peter Maurin knocking at her door: Maurin, the street philosopher who, Hennessy writes, "didn't say hello or goodbye, and every time he arrived . . . began talking where he had left off." He tells Dorothy he's been looking for her.

Maurin is the pivot character in this story. The unhinged hinge. More even than the birth of Tamar, Day's daughter (and Hennessy's mother), whose out-of-wedlock arrival in 1926 jump-started her conversion to Catholicism, it's the entrance of Maurin, shambling and riffing, that marks the great shift in the narrative of Dorothy Day.

Was *he* a saint? He was certainly a handful. A self-described French peasant, twenty years older than Day and with a well-travelled completely unplaceable cosmic-Celtic accent, Maurin showed up here and he showed up there and he talked and he talked. Was anyone listening? His ideas were a cranky hybrid of radical politics and Catholic social teaching, and he gave them to the air in extraordinary, rippling singsong. The word *communism*, he claimed, had been "stolen from the Church." Hennessy notes that some people found him ridiculous.

But not Day. Maurin's freakiness put her in the quantum realm, where things were in two places at once, and in his exhausting monologues she heard a program for action. With him she almost instantaneously founded the Catholic Worker Movement, the entity (Hennessy rather brilliantly calls it "a great American novel") to which she would henceforward give herself in serial gestures of the heart and commitments of the body. The Movement was first a newspaper—*The Catholic Worker,* which Day edited for forty-seven years—and then in short order a number of "houses of hospitality," some urban, some agrarian, all autonomous, dedicated to the provision of welcome (and food, and shelter) for the chronically unwelcome.

A lot of gas has been spewed recently—green, heavy, showbiz-wizard gas—about the disenfranchised person, the forgotten man. Well, Dorothy Day lived with the forgotten man, and he was a huge pain in the ass. His name was Mr. Breen, and during his residency at the Catholic Worker house on Mott Street he was a vituperative racist and a fire hazard. His name was also Mr. O'Connell, and as Mr. O'Connell he stayed for ten ill-natured years at

Maryfarm, the Catholic Worker's "agronomic university" in Newburgh, New York, slandering the other workers without mercy, hoarding the good tools, and generally making of himself "a scourge" (in Day's words) and "a sore trial" (in Hennessy's).

One gets the sense that Day reserved a special respect for these very difficult people, because it was with them—so thornily particular—that she was obliged to put flesh on all the blather about justice and generosity. This was, so to speak, where the rubber met the road. Loving Mr. Breen, loving Mr. O'Connell—that was work, the real stuff. Dealing with them day-to-day was moral jiujitsu. How tolerant could or should one be? At what point was one simply getting played, or (worse) indulging one's own goody-goodiness? "This turning the other cheek," wrote Day in her memoir *Loaves & Fishes*, "this inviting someone else to be a potential thief or murderer, in order that we may grow in grace. How obnoxious. In that case, I believe I'd rather be the striker than the meek one struck."

Meekness was not in her nature. Her obedience, her submission, to the Church and to the poor, was as headlong and headstrong in its way as her benders with Eugene O'Neill. And she was difficult herself, of course: a difficult example to follow.

In the New Testament, the arch-difficult person is John the Baptist: John, who comes striding out of the desert like a maniac, wearing his camel-hair loincloth and eating his locusts, shouting about Jesus. He's a frictional, almost intolerable figure, a challenge to domesticity and a challenge to author-ity, a man in whose presence complacency is impos-sible. With John there's no relaxing. No timeouts. Everything has to change. NOW.

So who's *your* John the Baptist? Your Dorothy Day? Your Mr. Breen? Complicated friend, can-tankerous relative, strong-willed child, impossible roommate . . . In your life, who is the person who demands the most of you, the best of you? They're talking to you right now, or not talking to you, and driving you mad, and stealing your tools, and using your shampoo, and insisting on a higher standard, and you can hear the locusts crunching between their teeth.

ODE TO HISTORY

If letters made sounds when we opened them, sounds expressive of their contents—if, from the freshly unsealed envelope, there rose a lover's sigh, or an alcoholic belch, or the briskly cleared throat of officialdom—the letters of Hunter S. Thompson would have released, I think, a noise like nearby gunfire. Like the local, jungle crackle of some kind of endless small-arms engagement. Pop, pop, pop, deep into the night.

I've been diving lately into the Thompson correspondence, via Douglas Brinkley's superb two-volume edition (*The Proud Highway* and *Fear and Loathing in America*) because I'm looking for answers. Answers to what? How about: to the huge, throbbing interrogative that is America in the 2020s. What is happening? Where's it going? How do you live in it?

The mid-sixties to the mid-seventies: that was Thompson's lean and scowling journalistic prime. "This fucking polarization," he laments to one correspondent, "has made it impossible to sell anything except hired bullshit or savage propaganda." But he was unstoppable. To research his book about the Hell's Angels he rode with his subjects for a year, getting a perfectly predictable stomping from them at the end of it; he was assaulted by Chicago cops at the Democratic National Convention in 1968; under wild duress he composed the immortal hallucination that is *Fear and Loathing in Las Vegas*; he covered the Watergate hearings. And while he didn't perfectly or lucidly see the future—didn't see us, didn't see now—he didn't exactly need to, because in his head he was already here.

The Thompson of the letters is not especially likeable. He is hard, compulsive, vengeful, nastily funny, and distended with the grandiosity of true desperation. Much of the correspondence is concerned with money: claiming expenses, chasing percentages, running from creditors, dunning and being dunned. American Express cancels his card; Thompson responds with sulphurous hauteur. "You bastards . . . You swine . . . My position today is the same as when this stupid trouble began. I'll pay the bill if my card is reinstated. Probably . . ."

Friends and enemies are hailed in the same lewd, far-end-of-the-bar voice. "Dear Tom . . ." he writes to Tom Wolfe. "You worthless scumsucking bastard." This is endearment. "Sidney . . ." he writes to Sidney Zion, an editor at *Scanlan's Monthly*, "You worthless lying bastard." This is abuse. (He goes on to tell Zion: "In ten years of dealing with all kinds of editors I can safely say I've never met a scumsucker like you.") And if he starts to repeat your first name—"You interest me, George." "Roscoe, old sport, are you still with me? Don't slink off . . ."—you're in trouble.

You could say that he had some very bad work habits. Or you could say that, over the course of a decade's writing and reporting, he basically donated his nervous system to America. Pre-1974 Thompson was mostly on Dexedrine; post-1974 he was mostly on cocaine. Booze was a constant. Many of the letters have that early-morning comedown feel: the whitening window and the wan vibes. "Why bother to make it right when nobody knows the difference anyway? . . . Christ I need a long hill and a cold morning sun to get me tuned again . . ." Drugs have their uses, but he saw with terrible clarity the bargain he was making, "wilfully trading" as he wrote to *Rolling Stone* editor Jann Wenner, "time Now for time Later."

He had a fastidious horror of the mass, the mob, the herd—be it a circle of leering bikers or a throng of inflamed Republican delegates. Watching Barry Goldwater address the Republican National Convention in 1964, he writes in one letter, "I recall . . . actually feeling afraid because I was the only person not clapping and shouting." Part of his brief, as saw it, was to track this incoming American atavism. "The Shits are in," he wrote after the Kennedy assassination. He loathed Nixon, although he made a friend of arch-Nixonian Pat Buchanan. ("We disagree so violently on almost everything that it's a real pleasure to drink with him.")

So the fissures ran deep, in his time as in ours. From the core, from the White House, disruption emanated. My hack brain keeps wanting to write "the parallels are uncanny"—but that's not it. These are not parallels; this is the same story. Thompson's letters impart the lesson: Fifty years on, this is the same America—the America of the raised night-stick, the cancelled credit card, the shuddering convention hall, the booming bike engine and the impossible dream.

ODE TO MY IDEA OF
QUANTUM PHYSICS

I am a particle. You are a wave.
    The presence of you affects how I behave.
(Old William Blake, he made the call:
    "The eye altering, alters all.")
We act on each other from afar.
    I think about you while I'm driving my car.
And all things around us hold their form
    while containing a species of cosmic storm.
The fridge and the floor and the Fourth of July
    are a seethe of equivocal nuclei.
Where's the white dwarf who set the timer?
    Could have been Ant-Man or Oppenheimer.
My atoms are your atoms, if you want them.
    And that's how it is in the realm of quantum.

ODE TO ADVICE COLUMNS

I will never, ever—short of some personality-altering event, moral or biological—write in to an advice column.

Why? Because I *read* them. I read them and I read them. When it comes to advice columns, that is, I'm strictly a voyeur. A peeping tom. And no quandary of the heart, no out-of-control kink, no high-stakes issue involving wedding invitations could impel me to be a participant.

Also: the problems are the same, now and forever. This is the point. This is who we are: the same dilemmas, the same misunderstandings. My boss is a pig. Why won't my stepdaughter say thank you? I married a frog—I thought he was a prince! And so on. They loop around, these problems, they rhythmically recur, albeit touched with the flavour of the times ("Help, My Pandemic Crush Feels So Real!"). How impossible it is, apparently, to be alive without getting in some huge bloody tangle. Is it freedom you want? Total libido blowout? The swingers have their problems too ("I Love My Poly Lifestyle, but the Constant Sex Has One Big Drawback").

And the problem of all problems, the old chest-nut: Why am I doing what I'm doing, when it's so obviously bad for me/my health/my family/the world? Saint Paul put this one best in his letter to the Romans: "For what I would, that do I not; but what I hate, that do I."

But I'm hooked. The habit was formed, for me, under slightly damp and Freudian conditions. It was in the family bathroom, in the pages of my mother's 1970s magazines—*Woman's Own*, *Woman's Weekly*, *Woman's Realm*—that I, a boy, first met them. The agony aunts. The problem-receivers. With what insight and asperity they sliced into the 200-word operettas laid before them, four or five to a page. And the women who wrote to them, who sought their advice—what complications they had. Adulterous explosions, erotic *ennui*, existential impatience, soul-death at the kitchen table. This deep and feminine world of *problems*—I couldn't get enough.

And I still can't. *Ask Polly, Dear Prudence* . . . I slurp it all up. Some of the letters I read with a gush of fellow feeling, some with icy snobbery. One of the keenest thrills for the problem-page addict is when an unreliable narrator shows up: an advice seeker whose own flaws, glaringly revealed in their letter, are still somehow obscure to them. We can barely wait for the columnist to straighten them out (*Your sister-in-law is quite right: you're a racist*).

It's not just the situations. The format itself is compulsive. The problem is expressed—and then, in a different tone, in a different font, the problem is solved. The advice is given. Setup, punchline. Tension, release. Yup, I'll keep reading. And reading. It's a little problem I have.

ODE TO MOOD SWINGS

I've had three since breakfast, and it's not even eleven a.m.

I've peaked (watching, from my kitchen window, a cat stare into a puddle), I've troughed (bad patch of writing), and I've bobbed in momentary equilibrium. And here you come again, my mood swing. Under the paving stones, the beach. Under the shining moment, the banana peel. Up, down, ding, dong, round and round and round . . . I think you might be wearing me out.

But I won't reject you. No, I won't repudiate you. I'm alive in America in the 2020s, and even-temperedness—emotional homeostasis—is neither attainable nor appropriate.

Besides, it's always been this way for you and me. *Chariots of Fire* laid it out when I was thirteen years old. "You, Aubrey, are my most complete man," says Harold Abrahams, the driven, prickly Olympic sprinter, to his friend Aubrey Montague. Harold is on the massage table, heavy with melancholic self-knowledge, getting a rubdown before his big race.

"You're brave," he tells Aubrey, in a sad, squished, horizontal voice. "Compassionate. Kind. A content man. That's your secret. Contentment! I'm 24 and I've never known it."

Great scene, no? Thus was the dialectic implanted in my young mind, in 1981. You could be a Harold in this world, grasping and yearning and prickling and perpetually mood-swinging—and with a shot at a gold medal—or you could be an Aubrey. And I knew which one I was.

But to be a Harold all the time, all over your surface area? What's it for, mood swingers? Why did nature do this to us?

I'll tell you why. Because she has her moods too, and we are her moody children. Light shifts across the face of that puddle-philosophical cat, the puddle changes color, and if I'm a failure today I might be a titan tomorrow—or in ten minutes. We are faithful, we who swing, to the humours of the day. That shaft of brightness, that spike of delight, will reliably fade. And at the base of the great gloom-cloud, beneath miles of obscurity, joy's little booster rockets are warming up already.

So swing, mood, swing. Flip us madly between the high note and the low. Because if we're extravagant in our reactions, we are frugal in our stimuli. This is our glory: it really doesn't take much to set us off. To get us flying again. A wet leaf, a guitar solo, a glad look. The warm orange of the Dunkin' Donuts logo, spied from a moving car . . . We are the lightweights; we are the cheap dates.

Hard to live with? Well, yes, possibly. I mean, sure. But if you're not enjoying me right now, can I ask for your patience? I'm like a London bus. There'll be another me along in a minute.

ODE TO BAKING

How they fascinated me, the beautiful bakers.

Strutting around in their aprons, making jokes, slapping and prodding and sniffing the rising dough, the ever-changing dough—amazing to me, the familiarity with which they touched it, the rough intimacy—with a fine aristocratic powdering of flour on their cheeks. And so brainy, too. "Hey Duncan, what does *apocryphal* mean?" Duncan, head deep in the industrially large mixing bowl from which he is cutting out heavy, claggy handfuls of just-mixed dough, replies instantly: "Of doubtful origin."

I can't do it in my kitchen. Or I could, I suppose, but I don't. No interest at all in baking bread at home. Nor do I give a toss, particularly, about the kind of bread I eat: white, brown, writhing with raw health or stuffed with additives, if you can toast it, I'm in. But I loved, loved, loved being a baker.

They trained me, God bless them. With forbearance and grumpiness, the bakers of Clear Flour Bread in Brookline, Massachusetts, turned me into one of their company. Was I any good? Ask my baguettes. Ask my olive rolls. Ask my goddamn Rustic Italian loaves. The bread judges the baker.

Baking is not mystical—it's scientific. Get the recipe right, do what you're supposed to do, and something pretty close to the desired outcome will be achieved. But of course it *is* mystical, like everything else. The condition of the baker's soul is alchemically involved. As above, so below. A jolly baker with a clear conscience is going to have a better bake, and produce tawnier and juicier bread, than his chafing, pissed-off colleague.

Also: did you know about wild airborne yeast? An invisible, activating agent that lives in the atmosphere like the grace of God? It's real.

The dough is on the move. At all times, all over the bakery, you feel the pressure of its mutability: it's rising, it's rising. Or it's collapsing, because you fucked up. It's a small window, the moment of perfect proofedness, plumpness, oven-readiness, fruition.

The baker touches the dough, tests it with her fingertips, feels the energy quiver under the fragile skin, the ballooning cells, the gassy bounce of its interior expansions, and makes the call. Too early and the bread will warp hysterically in the oven; too late and it'll lie there in protest, doing nothing.

Baguettes, are you ready to go? Did the baker cut you properly on the loader, giving you those three diagonal slashes, one after another, zip-zip-zip? If the razor went too deep, you'll fall apart, slump sadly open. And how much steam do you need, for a nice glossy crust? The baker hits the button, floods the oven deck with a gash of vapor—for how many seconds?

Now stand back, baker. You're as ancient as Egypt, and you're also Andy Warhol in an apron, mass-producing your art object. Baguettes in glowing dozens, repeating editions and series of baguettes, out of the great oven and onto the metal rack. How do they look? How do they sound? A field of grain right before the harvest will give off an audible creak or tick of readiness, as the loaded stalks gently rub against one another. At the other end of the process there's the fine, fuse-like crackle of a row of handsome, brittle baguettes, cooling on the rack.

ODE TO PULL-UPS

Who do I think I am, dangling off this bar?

I think I'm an ape. I think I'm an acrobat. I think I'm Jason Momoa. I think I'm a fifty-four-year-old man with a dodgy shoulder, experiencing—to the pound, to the ounce—the precise terms of my contract with gravity. That's one thing you can always say for the pull-up: you're lifting your own weight.

Its first cousin is of course the push-up. But the push-up has no verticality. A blur of ground, or of floor, bounces madly back and forth in front of your face. And besides, you're not pushing up your whole body weight, because you're propped on your feet. No, for the true self-heave, the full load of who you are, it has to be the pull-up.

You do pull-ups alone, very alone, but maybe a couple of your pull-up brothers are there too—grimly contemplative, walking in loose circles around the bar, shrugging and chewing and sighing. Pull-up talk is minimal and poetic. The other day I asked a big dude if I could jump in between his sets. He took out one earbud as I repeated the question. "Get at it," he said. "*Get* some."

Are you wondering how many I can do? I can do 3. I can do 60. I can do 102, in thirteen sets, over a period of two and a half days: sets of nine, sets of four, sets of minus two. As for technique, I've invented my own grip—I call it the French Press. The point is, I do them. I do pull-ups, and they never get any easier. Still the same flutter of dismay as I stare up at the metal bar. Still the same sensation of wrenched brain cells as I jump and grab and haul.

But the pull-up fixes me like no other exercise. It lifts me clear, literally, of my stews and stagnancies. It dramatizes my rising-above. Need a mood shifter, a circuit breaker? Do pull-ups. And do them outside. Nothing against gyms, or the pull-up bar installed in a doorway at home, but for the real pull-up effect you want to be hoisting yourself into the sky. At the moment of maximum effort, you want to be silhouetted against infinity.

Then you drop to the earth, the sturdy and ever-supportive earth. There it is, and there you are. Ready.

ODE TO NOT DRINKING II

Boozy tears,
boozy tears,
what are they really worth?
They come too easy.
They roll too greasy.
Let them fall and get lost in the earth.

ODE TO SLEEPING JESUS

Anxiety: What is it for you?

For me it's a high wind in the brain (with tumbling junk thoughts); rat-claw scratchiness around the nostrils; a sour drizzle at the back of the throat; a prickling, dying, going-bald feeling on the scalp; and a general sensation of having been projected out of the regular run of life and onto another plane of existence—one that far exceeds my nervous capacities. On this new plane everything is precarious, everything's in jeopardy, everything's naked and frail. Behind that tree—*that* one, over there—Death loudly sharpens his scythe: scrape, scrape, scrape.

All this, as philosophers have observed, is the price we pay for selfhood, at least as we're currently doing it. Our precious little boundaried finite earbud-wearing socially distanced twenty-first-century self, pitiful asterisk against a background of bottomless non-selfhood, of *not being there at all* . . . That's somewhat anxiety-producing.

So there's a storm on the Sea of Galilee. Jesus and the disciples are out there in a boat, out there on the

swinging-and-surging surface of the great unconscious ocean—which is basically the great Unconscious itself. Ever been smashed by a big wave?
Plucked from your feet, not far from the shore, and
mashed face-first into the gritty floor by a racing
heap of water with a delicately toppling crest? It's
phenomenally uninterested in who you are. You
feel this quite clearly as the weight pushes you
down, as the wave closes its fist on you: no venom
in it, nothing personal, just this veering, crushing,
glassily unthinking warp of sea strength in which
you happen to be caught. Identity—the fragile
shell, the craft, the little boat—is moot.

"And there arose a great storm of wind," as Mark's
Gospel has it, "and the waves beat into the ship, so
that it was now full." The disciples begin to freak
out: where's Jesus? Where is he, for crying out loud?
Shouldn't he be addressing this? But Jesus is asleep.
Very comfortably—and for the first and last time
in the Gospels—asleep. "And he was in the hinder
part of the ship, asleep on a pillow."

The disciples wake him with their fussing, Jesus (in
perhaps a sleep-thickened, slightly irritated voice)
"rebukes the wind," and the situation is resolved.
But this—the swatting down of the storm—is not
the power image in this scene. The power image is
sleeping Jesus, his lovely pillowed unperturbedness
as the waves pile up outside. This surface agitation

is nothing to him: His mind attaches to the depth, where the ocean sways on its quiet root. Afloat, preserved by his own fragility, he carries a secret that is no secret at all.

We can imagine him smiling as he sleeps.

ODE TO BANANAS

Don't rush it.

There's something so very consumer-friendly about a banana, from its helpfully tubular design to its easy-peel protective sheath to its no-teeth-necessary texture; something so easy, you just want to shove it into your face. It could be astronaut food: a specially engineered, hygienically sealed nutrition cylinder in high-visibility yellow. Even the taste is sort of space-age, sort of lab-redolent. Slurp it down, Major Tom. Reset your potassium levels and get back to your Martian rock samples. The peel will float off, anemone-like, in zero gravity.

But to slurp it down, to eat it heedlessly, is to waste the banana. It's to waste, first of all, the *duration* of a banana. Are you, like me, a wistful nonsmoker? Do you envy the smokers their philosophical interludes, their moments of drifting peace? Then eating a banana, slowly and reflectively, is the closest thing you're going to get to a cigarette break. Except better, because you can do it on public transportation. (Imagine, though, if there were smoking-style prohibitions on banana-eating: little knots of people outside office buildings, eating clandestine bananas . . .)

There's an orthodox, old-school surrealism to the banana: its cartoon yellowness, its absurd curvature, the fact that when we think about a banana, we think about it upside down. Because the banana grows upward, doesn't it, jostling for sunlight with its fellows—but in our mind, we reverse it. We put its broken stem on top, like a nose or a little horn, and so we create a strangeness around the banana. We put it in banana quotes.

But the banana is not, or not just, a free-floating, self-signifying object. It is fragile and organic: There are processes at work inside the banana. If battered or neglected, it will flush an angry dark brown. It will become its shadow. It should be a tarot card, one of the big ones: the Fool, the Hanged Man, and the Black Banana. Pull *that* card and change your life.

And you don't want to waste the taste, either—the green-turning-yellow flavour-wave of a banana. Me, I like a mottled one. The greener end of the spectrum is too fibrous for me, with too much of the wet-paint pinch of unripeness. Green bananas squeak when you peel them. I like a deep, mature yellow, with sunspots. That's a fulfilled banana, a mellow banana, a banana that's been around the block. It's loaded with the sugars of experience. It's in the last blaze of its bananahood.

Enjoy me now, it says with its banana grin. *I was created for your pleasure.*

ODE TO KEEPING IT SHORT

Have you run out of patience?

I don't mean just for now, relative to what's going on. I mean permanently. As in: it's all gone. Has that happened to you yet? It will. Because patience, one discovers, is not a virtue but a quantity. Like oil in the car or milk in the fridge. Not limitless and oceanic, but quite finite. I ran out years ago. All I have now is stamina. I can endure. Radiant with suppressed exasperation, I can hang in there.

Who used it up? Who exhausted my ratio of patience? Was it airports, traffic, moths, lost socks, dead batteries, daylight savings, toilet paper, to-do lists, the manifold obstructions, etc.? Yes, yes, all of the above. But mainly, I think, it was the bores.

I can certainly be boring. I watch *Seinfeld* every day while I'm eating my lunch. I have my themes. I have my tics. Reader, you may even have spotted some of them. But I'm not a bore. And when I meet a bore, having no patience to protect me, no buffer of tolerance, I'm on my mettle. I have to be. My sanity is at risk.

I'm talking about the real bores. The killer bores, the soul-slurping super-bores. The ones who, when they get their hooks in, cause a tickle of alarm in your brainstem, because they are a *threat*. The stultifiers, the hobbyhorsers, the buttonholers, the lecturers, the one-track minders. The gaseous raconteurs. The pop-eyed sermonizers. The drunks with their loops of sententiousness. The humourless ones. The sleepless semi-sociopaths who ask no questions, who have no ears, whose speech is a nonstop blare of exhalation. The *bores*.

So there goes my patience, destroyed by bores. And having no patience, I'm finding that pretty much everything these days goes on for too long.

Is it just me? I don't think it's just me. That's actually my chief article of writerly faith: if it's me, it's everybody. So I'm going to assume that we're all feeling this mortal irritability, this scrabbling under the coffin-lid that tells us *Get on with it*. Movies are too long; books are too long; meals are too long; anecdotes are too long; arguments are too long; soccer matches are too long; rock shows are too long; train rides are too long; sentences are too long; streets are too long; seasons are too long.

(Except autumn. Autumn has timing. The rolling crackle of colour, the brief spice in the air . . . Autumn goes out like the cello-notes at the end of Pink Floyd's "The Scarecrow"— too soon, too soon, with a yearning that points to eternity. We didn't get enough of it, and so it carries on inside us. Deep into winter, our minds are printed with the flame of autumn.)

My friend Josh is almost as non-patient as me. His passion for economy, he maintains, is the result of an extended adolescent exposure, in Boston, Massachusetts, to American hardcore punk rock. Once you know what can be achieved, in other words, how much air can be shifted, how much feeling ignited, in one minute and sixteen seconds—once you've seen Bad Brains do "The Regulator"—there's no going back.

I once saw a band made up of outpatients from a mental health program in Hackney, east London. They did one song, or half a song. *You've got WHITE LEGS* bayed the shaven-headed singer over a clanking doomy post-punk groove. *I wanna SLEEP WITH YOU . . . You've got LOVELY LEEEEGS . . . I wanna FUUUUUUCK YOU . . .* Then he shouted "All coppers are BASTARDS!" and kicked over the mic stand and either dived or fell off the stage. It was the best thing I'd ever seen. The room shone. The room pulsed with a happily astounded silence; for about thirty seconds, we were all living in a new society.

Here's the advice that I, well-cooked old ham, always give to first-time public speakers: "Keep it short. No one ever came up to anybody at the end of a speech and said *That was great. I just wish it had been ten minutes longer.*" Seriously, keep it short. Keep it tight. Rambling eulogist, windy professor, hoarse and tasteless best man—sit down, for fuck's sake. Brevity is sacred. Life, left to itself, will dribble and dawdle along, eventually using up the available options. But make a hole, leave a bit of a vacuum, and there's room for possibility.

Get in and get out. Be artistic. Be righteous. Be tighteous. Be Bad Brains. Be white legs. And you'll hear it, way out there beyond whatever room or hall or tent you're in: a rustling and a pattering, a wash of cosmic approbation—the spaces between the stars applauding you.

ODE TO LOW EXPECTATIONS

So there I was, staring at my mug of tea.

It was 1993. I was sitting over a plate of eggs in the New Piccadilly Cafe in Soho, London. Things— apart from the eggs, which were delicious—were not going well. As a man, as a person, as a unit of society, I was barely functioning. More acutely, I was having panic attacks, in an era when people didn't yet say *panic attack*. They just said *Oh dear*. As far as I was concerned, I was going insane.

I took a despairing slurp of tea, put the mug back down. As I did so, as the side of my hand touched the Formica tabletop, I felt the radiant heat from where the mug had been resting a second before. Or more accurately, I registered it. I wasn't really *feeling* anything in those days.

So through my private cerebral drizzle, the contin- uous, joy-cancelling brain-rain that was my mental reality at the time, I noted it: a pleasant sensation. Energy, life, jiggling molecules, the world.

It was trying to get through to me.

And oddly enough, it did. At that moment, from the fire of generosity at the heart of the real, I got the message. And the message was this: One day—not today, but one day—you'll be able to simply appreciate what's in front of you. The tea, the cafe, London, this little lens of warmth on the table. One day, this will be enough. So stick around, why don't you.

Strive for excellence by all means. My God, *please* strive for excellence. Excellence alone will haul us out of the hogwash. But lower the bar, and keep it low, when it comes to your personal requirements. Gratification? Satisfaction? Having your needs met? Fool's gold. If you can get a buzz of animal cheer from the rubbishy sandwich you're eating, the daft movie you're watching, the highly difficult person you're talking to, you're in business. And when trouble comes, you'll be fitter for it.

"Reality is B plus," says my friend Carlo. I'd probably give it an A minus, but I take his point. "There lives a dearest freshness deep down things," wrote Gerard Manley Hopkins. But there also lives a dearest shoddiness. We're half-finished down here, always building and collapsing, rigging up this and that, dropped hammers and flapping tarps everywhere. Revise your expectations downward, and then downward again. Extend forgiveness to your idiot friends; extend forgiveness to your idiot self. Make it a practice. Come to rest in actuality.

ACKNOWLEDGMENTS

The author wishes to thank his agent Andrew Stuart, his editor Dan Gerstle, Jeff Goldberg at *The Atlantic*, Zeba Arora at Norton, and everybody who made the production of this book possible.

The following were previously published in *The Atlantic*: "Ode to America," "Ode to Coming Round," "Ode to Hotel Rooms," "Ode to Taking It Seriously," "Ode to Balloons," "Ode to Giving People Money," "Ode to the Pandemic," "Ode to Crying Babies," "Ode to Chewing Gum," "Ode to My Flip Phone," "Ode to Rushing," "Ode to the Unexpected Reversal," "Ode to BBQ Chips," "Ode to the Left Hand," "Ode to Insomnia," "Ode to Middle Age," "Ode to Not Meditating," "Ode to Getting It Wrong," "Ode to Small Talk," "Ode to Squirrels," "Ode to Naps," "Ode to My Thesaurus," "Ode to Running in Movies," "Ode to Cold Showers," "Ode to Electricity," "Ode to Procrastination," "Ode to Difficult People," "Ode to History," "Ode to Advice Columns," "Ode to Mood Swings," "Ode to Baking,"

"Ode to Pull-Ups," "Ode to Bananas," and "Ode to Low Expectations."

The following were previously published in *Slate*: "Ode to Finding Out What You're Here For," "Ode to the Everything That Isn't Me," and "Ode to Luck."

The following was previously published in *The New York Times*: "Ode to Bad Reviews."

The following was previously published in *Boston Magazine*: "Ode to Sitting There."